Anonymous

Report of the Commission to Investigate the Public Charitable and Reformatory Interests and Institutions of the Commonwealth

Anonymous

Report of the Commission to Investigate the Public Charitable and Reformatory Interests and Institutions of the Commonwealth

ISBN/EAN: 9783337296551

Printed in Europe, USA, Canada, Australia, Japan

Cover: Foto ©Suzi / pixelio.de

REPORT OF THE COMMISSION

TO INVESTIGATE

The Public Charitable and Reformatory Interests and Institutions of the Commonwealth.

FEBRUARY, 1897.

BOSTON:
WRIGHT & POTTER PRINTING CO., STATE PRINTERS,
18 POST OFFICE SQUARE.
1897.

Commonwealth of Massachusetts.

STATE HOUSE, BOSTON, February 1, 1897.

To His Excellency the Governor and the Honorable Council.

The undersigned, members of the Commission created by the following Resolve —

[CHAP. 60.]

RESOLVE TO AUTHORIZE THE APPOINTMENT OF A COMMISSION TO INVESTIGATE THE CHARITABLE AND REFORMATORY INTERESTS AND INSTITUTIONS OF THE COMMONWEALTH.

Resolved, That the governor, by and with the advice of the council, be and he is hereby authorized to appoint a commission, consisting of three persons, to investigate the public charitable and reformatory interests and institutions of the Commonwealth; to inquire into the expediency of revising the system of administering the same and of revising all existing laws in regard to pauperism and insanity, including all laws relating to pauper settlements; and furthermore to inquire into the relation of pauperism and insanity to crime, with a view to securing economy and efficiency in the care of the poor and insane in this Commonwealth. Said commission may employ a stenographer, shall have power to send for persons and papers, and may incur such expenses and receive such compensation for their services as the governor and council may determine. Said commission shall submit its report in print, with a bill or bills, if practicable, to the governor and council before the first day of February in the year eighteen hundred and ninety-seven. [*Approved April 13, 1896.*

herewith present their report.

WILLIAM F. WHARTON.
CHARLES F. FOLSOM.
DAVIS R. DEWEY.

Report of the Commission on

Charitable and Reformatory Interests and Institutions.

The commission organized on Monday, May 11, 1896, and began hearings on May 26, 1896. We were desirous of conferring with every person or association of persons who could furnish any information upon the subjects referred to us in the resolution under which we were organized. We therefore invited all persons informed and interested in these subjects to present their views. We held thirty-eight private hearings, and advertised and held two public hearings in June. We also advertised in newspapers published in different parts of the Commonwealth on November 11, 14, 18, 21 and 28, 1896, to the effect that we were prepared to give hearings, either public or private, to any persons who had any matters to present for our consideration. To these notices no response was made asking for public hearings. A few persons requested to be heard privately, and they were so heard.

We have, in conformity with what we believed to be the intention of the Legislature, included in our investigation questions arising as to the system of administration of the penal as well as the charitable and reformatory institutions. We have been led, moreover, to do this because the subjects were so closely connected that they were often difficult to separate in our deliberations. We have endeavored to make the recommendations hereinafter set out conform to the best development not only of the institutions themselves but also of the general charitable and reformatory interests of the Commonwealth. We have considered the existing laws in regard to pauperism and insanity and the laws relating to pauper settlements. The time allowed us has not permitted our inquiring into the large subject of the relation of pauperism and insanity to crime in such manner as to present any views that we feel would be of value to the Commonwealth. We suggest that, if it be deemed best that an inquiry should be made into this subject, the work be assigned to some other board or commission, perhaps to the State Board of Insanity and the State Board of Charity acting together, if created in accordance with the recommendations of this report.

We concluded, early in our work, that, in view of the time fixed for our making a report, it was not the expectation of the Legislature that we should undertake a minute investigation of the several State institutions; and we have consequently devoted ourselves to the examination and consideration of the system of administering the institutions and of the laws affecting them, and the general interests referred to in the resolve under which we were appointed, with a view to presenting such changes in these matters as might recommend themselves to us from our own observation and study and from the suggestions made to us by those persons who were experienced and interested.

We have consulted with the State Board of Lunacy and Charity and with their officers upon several occasions, and we have given hearings to the trustees of the Lyman and Industrial Schools and to the superintendent of the former, the trustees and the superintendents of the State Almshouse and the State Farm, the trustees and superintendent of the Massachusetts Hospital for Dipsomaniacs and Inebriates, the trustees and the superintendents of the several lunatic hospitals in the Commonwealth, the Commissioners of Prisons, the warden of the State Prison, the superintendents of the Massachusetts Reformatory and of the Reformatory Prison for Women, the Children's Aid Society, the Massachusetts Medical Society, the Boston Medico-Psychological Society, the Massachusetts Homœopathic Medical Society, the Massachusetts Prison Association, the Massachusetts Association of Relief Officers, the Institutions Commissioner of the city of Boston, the sheriffs and county commissioners of the several counties in the Commonwealth and the probation officers of Boston and Springfield. We have offered opportunities to the mayors of the different cities of the Commonwealth to consult with us, and many valuable suggestions have been offered by those officials. We have further communicated with the Chief justice and justices of the superior court and with the Chief justice and justices of the municipal court of the city of Boston, and the judges of the other municipal, police and district courts of the Commonwealth, from many of whom we have received most valuable suggestions.

We have moreover consulted with every person individually who desired to offer any suggestions upon the subjects which we have had under consideration.

We submit herewith our recommendations and suggestions.

JUVENILE WARDS.

According to the report of the State Board of Lunacy and Charity of 1895, the number of juvenile wards of the Commonwealth at the close of the official year was 2,593. These juvenile wards may be classified in the following manner: —

First. — Juvenile offenders, being minors between the ages of seven and seventeen years, who are guilty of some crime or misdemeanor, and who are committed to the Lyman School for Boys, to the Industrial School for Girls or to the custody of the State Board of Lunacy and Charity.

Second. — Children between three and sixteen years of age, who, by reason of orphanage or of the poverty, neglect, crime, drunkenness or other vice of parents, are growing up without education or salutary control, and in circumstances exposing them to lead idle and dissolute lives, or are dependent upon public charity. These children, if they have no known settlement in the Commonwealth, shall be, or if their place of legal settlement has not within its control any institution in which they may be lawfully maintained, may be committed to the State Board of Lunacy and Charity. Those of them who have a known settlement are committed to the overseers of the poor of the city or town in which they have such settlement, except in Boston; and if they have a settlement in Boston, they are committed to the Institutions Commissioner of the said city.

Third. — Abandoned, neglected or dependent infants, under three years of age.

By the same report it appears that, of the juvenile offenders, 264 were at the Lyman School for Boys; 111 were at the State Industrial School for Girls; 582 were outside the schools, but in the custody and control of the trustees of the Lyman and Industrial Schools, and placed out, or boarded out by them in their own or other families; and 325 were in the care, custody and control of the State Board of Lunacy and Charity, making a total of 1,282 juvenile offenders.

Of the so-called dependent and neglected children, including the infants, there were 1,311 in the care and custody of the State Board of Lunacy and Charity. If we add to this last number the 325 juvenile offenders in their care, we find that there was at the close of the official year of 1895 a total of 1,636 juvenile wards of the Commonwealth who were directly under the care, custody and control of the State Board of Lunacy and Charity, and were taken care of by the in-door and out-door departments of the Board. From this it appears that almost two-thirds of the juvenile wards of the Commonwealth are now in the direct care, custody and control of the State Board of Lunacy and Charity, and over them there is no supervisory authority except such as the Board chooses to exercise itself; while over those in the custody and under the control of the trustees of the Lyman and Industrial Schools the Board exercises supervisory powers.

We believe that it requires no argument to show that the same Board cannot in the nature of things undertake the care of a class of State wards, and likewise occupy a position of independent criticism of its own work in this direction. The only effective supervision is that which is exercised by a Board, or by officers, who have no part in the duties to be supervised; and the object of supervision — and this is specially applicable to all charitable work — is to inquire into the work done, to suggest improvements and to correct evils which may be found to exist.

Supervision by a distinct and separate authority of all work done by officers having the care and custody of any class of State wards seems to have been the policy of the Commonwealth, as indicated by the course of legislation. All the State institutions having the care of State paupers and juvenile offenders — for instance, the State Almshouse, the State Farm, the Lyman School for Boys, the Industrial

School for Girls and all the State lunatic hospitals and asylums — are governed by boards of trustees, and are subject to the supervision of the State Board of Lunacy and Charity. The three exceptions in this regard seem to be the care and custody of neglected and dependent children and of certain juvenile offenders, of insane paupers boarded in families and of the Indians who have not acquired settlements in any town in the Commonwealth.

The care of the Indians, which was given to the Board in 1869 (see P. S., c. 86, § 23), is of so small importance that it can well be left with the State Board of Charity if created.

The care of the boarded-out insane was given to the State Board of Health, Lunacy and Charity in 1885 (St. 1885, c. 385), and the number of insane persons boarded out under its provisions at the time of the last report of the State Board of Lunacy and Charity was 142. Our recommendations upon this subject are found in another part of this report, where we deal with the subject of the insane.

The care of the neglected and dependent children and of certain juvenile offenders by the Board seems to be now the only important exception to the generally recognized rule above stated. Efforts have been made from time to time, as is learned from an inspection of the legislation of the Commonwealth, to remove this exception.

The powers given by statutory enactments to the "Board of Commissioners in Relation to Alien Passengers and State Paupers," from which Board has originated the present State Board of Lunacy and Charity, were of a supervisory and *quasi*-judicial nature. That Board was not given the custody and control of any class of State paupers. The executive officers whose work was supervised were the superintendents of alien passengers created in 1848 (St. 1848, c. 313). At that date the State paupers were taken care of by the several cities and towns in which they were found, and the expense of their support was paid for by the Commonwealth. The object of the legislation with reference to the alien passengers and State paupers was mainly to prevent the advent into the country of aliens likely to become a burden on the State, and to secure adequate indemnity at the time of their arrival against the event of their becoming such burdens.

In 1856 (St. 1856, c. 294), the Board was reorganized and the name changed to the "Board of Commissioners on Alien Passengers and State Paupers," and all the powers and duties of the former Board were conferred upon the new Board. It was further provided by § 3 of the above statute that the commissioners "shall have the same power to bind, as apprentices, minors who are inmates of a hospital at Rainsford Island, and the same powers, respectively, in relation to any State paupers who are now or may hereafter become inmates of the same, or of either of the lunatic asylums in this Commonwealth, and their property, if they have any, or any property left by them in case of their decease, as are by law vested in towns and in the overseers of the poor in towns, in reference to those paupers who are in any way supported or relieved by towns." This gave the Board the entire care and control of the class of State paupers therein described, and seems to have been the first occasion when the Board was given the care, custody and control of any class of State wards. But this legislation was not, it seems, acceptable for long; for, although these provisions of law were continued in Gen. Stats., c. 71, §§ 1–10, by St. 1863, c. 240, the said Board of Commissioners on Alien Passengers and State Paupers was abolished, and the Board of State Charities and the offices of general agent of State charities and of secretary of the Board of State Charities were created; and by § 6 of said act it was provided that all the duties then required by law to be performed by the incumbents of the offices which were abolished should be performed by the secretary and general agent therein provided for, subject to the control and direction of the Board of State Charities; thus transferring to the officers above named the control and custody of the paupers described in St. 1856, c. 294, § 3. The general agent and secretary were appointed by the Governor, with the advice and consent of the Council; and, although they were members *ex officio* of the Board of State Charities, all their work was subject in fact only to the supervision of the Board. They were expressly given all the executive and administrative powers to perform and duties to fulfil, and the Board could not enforce its decision or wishes, if adverse to their action, by their removal or in any other effective manner.

The duties of the Board are thus described in St. 1863, c. 240, § 4: "They shall investigate and supervise the whole system of the public, charitable and correctional institutions of the Commonwealth, and shall recommend such changes and additional provisions as they may deem necessary for their economical and efficient administration. They shall have full power to transfer pauper inmates from one charitable institution or lunatic hospital to another, and for this purpose to grant admittances and discharges to such pauper inmates, but shall have no power to make purchases for the various institutions." So, too, the visiting agent of the Board of State Charities (St. 1870, c. 359), whose duty it was to visit all the children maintained wholly or in part by the State, or indentured or placed in charge of any person by any State institution, ward or officer of the Commonwealth, was appointed by the Governor, and was an independent officer, whose duties were prescribed by statute.

In 1870, by the same statute as that which created the visiting agent of the Board of State Charities, the Board was authorized, under conditions set out in the statute, to indenture certain children therein specified, "or otherwise provide for his or her maintenance during minority, or for a less time;" and it is from that time that the large control of juvenile wards of the Commonwealth has grown gradually to be an important part of the work of the present State Board of Lunacy and Charity. Reference to the reports of that Board from year to year will show how the number of juvenile wards of the Commonwealth has grown from small to large proportions; and the abolition in 1895 of the State Primary School at Monson has already been, and will probably be, the cause of many more children being placed in the care and custody and under the control of the State Board of Lunacy and Charity, if it continues to exist as at present.

Department for Children.

We believe that the work of caring for the State children has grown to such proportions that the time has come to recur, in this instance as well as in others where State paupers are cared for, to the old principle of supervision, properly so called, and to create separate departments, one to have the care, custody and control of the juvenile wards of the State, and the other to exercise supervisory powers in relation to the work performed. We therefore recommend the creation of a department which shall have the care, custody and control of all the juvenile wards of the Commonwealth who are not in the State Almshouse, or the Lyman School for Boys, or the State Industrial School for Girls. We further recommend that such department be subject to the supervision of the State Board of Charity, as it may be created under the recommendation of this report.

The constitution of this department for the care of juvenile wards of the Commonwealth is a question of some difficulty; but we believe that, in view of the peculiar nature of the work it has to perform, it would be better to place at the head of that department a Board of Trustees of seven persons, one of whom shall be selected from the Board of Trustees of the Lyman and Industrial Schools, and three of whom at least shall be women. This Board would be similar to the other Boards having charge of the different charitable institutions and lunatic hospitals of the Commonwealth. The advantages of such a Board of Trustees, as compared with a single head, are apparent, when it is considered that, in the care of the juvenile wards of the Commonwealth, educational and other questions of much difficulty arise, which can be better treated by the combined judgment of several persons, devoted to and interested in the subject, than by the judgment of any one man or woman.

We recommend that all the juvenile wards of the Commonwealth who are now under the control of the trustees of the Lyman and Industrial Schools, outside the schools, shall be placed under the care and custody of the department above suggested, and that in future, when in the judgment of the trustees of the Lyman and Industrial Schools any juvenile ward can be better cared for outside the schools, such ward should be placed in the custody and under the control of the said department. In recommending that one of the members of the board of trustees of the above-named schools should likewise be a member of the board of trustees of the Department for Children we intend that there shall be sympathetic co-operation between the two boards.

The new department might be named the "Department for Children," and should be entrusted with all the powers and duties relating to the care, custody and control of children now exercised by and incumbent upon the State Board of Lunacy and Charity, and performed by it through the departments for the in-door and out-door poor, as organized at present. It should have full power to appoint such agents and other subordinate officers as it deems fit, and to fix their compensation, subject to the approval of the Governor and Council; and to it should be transferred the licensing of boarding-houses for infants and the prosecution of cases of violation of the infant-boarding law. Moreover, the agents and other officers of the department should be authorized by law to serve all criminal process in juvenile cases, when requested to do so by the court or magistrate and also to act as probation officers when requested by the court or magistrate; and should be given the custody of the child during the whole, or any part, of the term of the probation, and should further be authorized at any time during the period of probation to take the child without warrant and surrender him or her to the court or magistrate, by whom the probation is allowed. These last suggestions are made with a view to allow a child to be committed to the care of the Department for Children for an indeterminate period, thus avoiding the necessity, which has heretofore often occurred, of committing a child, guilty of a small offence, to one of the State institutions or to the State Board of Lunacy and Charity during his or her minority.

We also recommend that juvenile offenders under twelve years of age, who, as the law stands at present, cannot be committed to a jail, house of correction or to the State Workhouse, for non-payment of a fine, may be committed to the care and supervision of the Department for Children for a term not exceeding thirty days. It is easy to see, as the law stands at present, that such children practically go unpunished; and we believe that supervision, such as that suggested, might have a desirable effect.

We further recommend that children under fourteen years of age, who are held as witnesses, should not be committed to a jail, but should be given into the custody of the Department for Children until such time as he or she is needed to give his or her testimony. This will be the case where a child is unable to furnish bail for examination, or trial. (See St. 1882, c. 127, § 2; 1886, c. 101, § 4.)

We are aware that the creation of this Department for Children may involve a somewhat larger expenditure of money by the Commonwealth than the system under which the children are now cared for. It is difficult, if not impossible, to foresee exactly how large the amount of the increase may be; but there is every reason to believe that the advantages to the juvenile wards of the Commonwealth in the adoption of the new system will more than counterbalance any such additional burden which may be thrown upon the Commonwealth for their care and support. Moreover, we see no reason to anticipate that the new system, if properly conducted, will be an expensive one.

We feel confident that the persons selected by the appointing power to fill the positions of trustees of this department will be amply able to deal with the questions which are presented to their consideration and action. This Commonwealth stands well in the vanguard of those States of the Union which have adopted the most approved methods for the care and treatment of their poor and offending children, and, when we indicate below certain subjects as worthy of special attention, we are aware that we are only reiterating what has already often been stated before by the official authorities of the Commonwealth or by those who have at heart the subject with which we are now dealing.

More good can be done to juvenile offenders by proper

intervention at the time when the question first arises of what shall be done with them, than at any other period of their career. This question originates before some court or magistrate of the Commonwealth, before whom the children are brought, to be disposed of as is thought proper under the law. Great care should be had to have proper officers representing the Department for Children at every such hearing, in order that they may investigate into the antecedents of each child brought before the court or magistrate, and be able to advise fully as to his or her future disposition.

Other subjects which will undoubtedly engage the attention of both the State Board of Charity and the Department for Children, if created, are, whether there are not too frequent commitments by the courts and magistrates to institutions in cases where children might be better given to the care of the Department for Children; the selection and training of visitors for children boarded or placed out, and the frequency of visitation upon such children; whether or not the attention of the probation officers should be directed to children more than it is at present; the avoidance of the detention of boys and girls in houses of correction; the co-operation of the State authorities with the overseers of the poor in all cases where children have settlements, and the advisability of the codification of the laws which relate to children.

Truancy.

The subject of truancy is now under consideration by the State Board of Education, and a report upon the subject, called for by Res. 1895, c. 47, has already been made to the General Court. Upon receipt of that report the General Court last year adopted a resolve directing the State Board of Education to report to the next General Court a plan for carrying into execution the recommendations submitted by said Board in its report upon the subject. We feel that it was the manifest intention of the General Court that we should be relieved of the consideration of this subject, and that it should be dealt with by the State Board of Education;

and we therefore have no recommendations to make upon the subject except in one aspect in which the matter has been brought particularly to our notice in the course of our examination of the treatment of neglected children and juvenile offenders. The county commissioners of the several counties are authorized, by P. S., c. 220, § 18, to establish in each county a house of reformation, to which offenders under the age of sixteen years may be sentenced in all cases punishable with imprisonment, or for non-payment of fine, or fine and costs; and by § 19 of the same chapter, cities and towns in each county may assign such house of reformation as the institution provided for persons convicted of being habitual truants, or of wandering about the streets and public places of a city or town, having no lawful employment or business, not attending school and growing up in ignorance. The collection of truants and juvenile offenders in the same building is unfortunate, and a change should be made in the law in this respect, so that the two classes of children shall be kept apart. We also recommend, in conformity with the suggestion of the State Board of Lunacy and Charity contained in their report for 1895, that the law relating to neglected children be so amended that such children shall not be sent to the truant schools, as is possible under the existing law (St. 1894, c. 498, §§ 19, 28).

Intermediate Reformatory.

Our attention has been brought to the need of an intermediate reformatory for boys who are too old to be sent under the law to the Lyman School for Boys, and yet seem to be too young in years to be advantageously sent to the Concord Reformatory. It is somewhat difficult to ascertain accurately the number of boys that could be sent to such an intermediate institution, if created; but we suggest that the State Board of Charity, if created, together with the Commissioners of Prisons, direct their attention to the consideration of this matter, and if, in their estimation, the number of boys who would be advantageously affected by the creation of such a reformatory is sufficient to authorize the expenditure of money by the Commonwealth in its construction, we should recommend that it be done. Accommodations for such an institution might be provided by the construction of a new building, or by the setting off of a portion of some one of the institutions already existing.

Bills are herewith submitted, incorporating the above suggestions as to juvenile wards, and are presented in Appendix A.

THE INSANE.

According to the report of the State Board of Lunacy and Charity for the year 1895, there were on September 30 of that year in the several State lunatic hospitals and insane asylums, at the State Farm and State Almshouse, the following number of insane persons, including 20 dipsomaniacs and 10 voluntary patients: —

Worcester Lunatic Hospital,	961
Taunton Lunatic Hospital,	846
Northampton Lunatic Hospital,	546
Worcester Insane Asylum,	447
Danvers Lunatic Hospital,	948
Westborough Insane Hospital,	567
State Farm,	244
State Almshouse,	473
	5,032

Of this number, 523 were private patients, the cost of whose support was paid for out of private funds, leaving 4,509 patients the cost of whose support was borne by the cities and towns in which the insane persons had settlements, and by the Commonwealth when the insane persons had no settlements.

Besides the above hospitals, there is the Massachusetts Hospital for Dipsomaniacs and Inebriates, established by St. 1889, c. 414, of which there were at the time named 129 inmates; the Medfield Insane Asylum, established by St. 1892, c. 425, for the chronic insane, to which the chronic insane in the hospitals above enumerated are being transferred as the buildings are ready for occupancy; and the Massachusetts Hospital for Epileptics, established by St. 1895, c. 438.

All of the above institutions are governed by boards of trustees, who appoint all subordinate officers.

Moreover, besides the insane persons above enumerated in the State hospitals, asylums and institutions, there were at the time named 527 patients in the Boston Lunatic Hospital, 204 in corporate or private asylums, 142 boarded in private families in charge of the State Board of Lunacy and Charity, and approximately 863 in the care of the overseers of the poor of the several cities and towns of the Commonwealth, making a total of 5,905 insane persons under medical supervision, and about 863 in charge of the overseers of the poor. All of the patients in the corporate or private asylums, 60 in municipal asylums and 17 of those boarded in families under State control were supported by private funds.

Over all of these persons and of the institutions of which they are inmates the State Board of Lunacy and Charity has supervisory powers.

The Board is required to report annually to the governor and council a properly classified and tabulated statement of the receipts and expenses for that year of each of the several State institutions under its charge, and a corresponding classified and tabulated statement of their estimates for the year ensuing; and it is required to express its opinion as to the necessity or expediency of the appropriation in accordance with the estimates. It is also required to present such suggestions and recommendations as it may deem fit, relating to the work of the several institutions and to the general interests of insane persons throughout the State. It is also required to prepare, from the returns made by the overseers of the poor, tables of all the pauper insane supported by towns, and to print in its annual report the most important information thus obtained. It is authorized to transfer any insane pauper from the State lunatic hospitals to the insane ward of the State Almshouse, and from one State lunatic hospital to another, and to transfer and commit inmates from the other State institutions to the State lunatic hospitals and asylums, and may under certain conditions transfer inmates of private asylums to other private asylums and to the State lunatic hospitals. It has also power to send insane paupers away to another State, or to the place where they belong.

It is, moreover, obliged at least once in every year to visit all places where State paupers are supported, and to ascertain, from actual examination and inquiry, whether the laws with respect to such paupers are properly observed, particularly in relation to such as are able to labor; and is obliged also to give such directions as will insure correctness in the returns required in relation to the paupers; and it has, generally, the same powers relating to the State paupers who are inmates of the lunatic hospitals in the State, and their property, as are vested in towns and overseers of the poor in reference to paupers supported or relieved by towns. It is authorized, when it has reason to believe that any insane person not curable is deprived of remedial treatment and is confined in an almshouse or other place, to make application for the commitment of such person to a State hospital. It shall by itself or its agent visit every asylum for the insane established by any city under St. 1884, c. 234, and it has the same power of removal and transfer of the inmates of these asylums which it has of those of other hospitals or asylums for the insane. It has the power to enforce the law regulating the districts from which insane persons can be committed to the State hospitals, and it has the care and custody of the insane who are boarded in families. It is also obliged, by itself or its agents, to visit and inspect every private asylum, or receptacle for the insane, at least once in every six months.

It has, moreover, power to act as Commissioners of Lunacy, with power to investigate the question of the insanity and condition of any person committed to any lunatic hospital or asylum, public or private, or restrained of his liberty by reason of his alleged insanity, at any place in the Commonwealth; and has power to discharge any such person, if in its opinion such person is not insane, or can be cared for, after such discharge, without danger to others and with benefit to himself.

These powers and duties, entrusted to the State Board

of Lunacy and Charity, have been of gradual growth, beginning with the Board of Commissioners in Relation to Alien Passengers and State Paupers, established in 1851, and extending through all the period included between that year and the present time. It would be interesting, if we had the space and time, to trace this growth through the statutes; but it is more to the point, for our present purpose, to draw attention to the accumulation of work in relation to the insane wards of the Commonwealth and to the subject of insanity generally, that now rests upon the Board and its duly appointed agents.

Moreover, in this connection it should be noted that the State lunatic hospitals consisted for many years of only the Worcester, Taunton and Northampton hospitals. The Danvers Hospital and the Worcester Insane Asylum were both established in 1877; the Westborough Insane Hospital in 1884; the Medfield Asylum in 1892; and in 1895 the State Asylum for Insane Criminals at Bridgewater; and latterly there has been created the Massachusetts Hospital for Epileptics and the Massachusetts Hospital for Dipsomaniacs and Inebriates, both of which institutions would seem to require somewhat the same sort of general supervision and care as the lunatic hospitals and asylums; and the duties of the State Board, prescribed especially for lunatic hospitals and asylums, would seem equally applicable to them. The number of State lunatic hospitals and asylums, therefore, properly so called, which have come under the supervision of the State Board of Lunacy and Charity, has since 1877 more than doubled. The increased powers and duties of the Board in this and other regards and its added powers and duties as Commissioners of Lunacy, with all that may be involved in the examination of the sanity and condition of any person committed to any lunatic hospital or asylum, be it a public one or a private one, or of any person who is restrained of his liberty, on the ground of his alleged insanity, at any place within the Commonwealth, call for an amount of work to be performed by the Board which was hardly contemplated at the time that the supervision of the lunatic hospitals and of the insane poor was first given to it.

The importance of the work which devolves upon the State Board of Lunacy and Charity, in this direction alone, can hardly be exaggerated, and the possibilities of the further development of the work, both in a scientific and a practical direction, are worthy of the most careful attention. That work we believe is sufficient in itself to authorize the creation of an independent Board to carry it out effectively.

The same Board, or department, should not be called upon to perform duties respectively so important in themselves and so little related to each other as those regarding the insane wards of the Commonwealth and the general subject of insanity, and those relating to the charitable institutions and the charitable interests of the Commonwealth. We believe that the time has come to set apart duties which are sufficient in themselves to occupy a department created for their express fulfilment.

STATE BOARD OF INSANITY.

We therefore recommend that a State Board of Insanity be created, consisting of five persons, who shall each hold office for the term of five years. They shall be appointed by the governor, with the advice and consent of the council; two of them shall be expert in insanity, and shall devote their whole time to the performance of their duties as members of the Board, and shall each receive a salary of $5,000 a year and his actual expenses. The other members of the Board shall receive no salaries, but shall be paid only for their necessary expenses actually incurred in the performance of their duties. The Board also shall have the power to appoint such agents and subordinate officers as it may deem requisite, and to fix their salaries, subject to the approval of the governor and council.

We recommend that to this Board shall be transferred all the powers relating to the subject of insanity which are now exercised by the State Board of Lunacy and Charity, and that the Board shall exercise the same powers of supervision, transfer, and otherwise over the Massachusetts Hospital for Epileptics and the Massachusetts Hospital for Dipsomaniacs and Inebriates, which it will have in regard to hospitals and asylums for the insane, when the transfer which we recommend above shall have been made. The Massachusetts School for the Feeble-Minded and the Hospital Cottages for Children, chiefly epileptic, would naturally also come under the supervision of this Board. It shall visit at least once in every year all places where insane poor are supported, and ascertain from actual examination and inquiry whether the laws with respect to such insane poor are properly observed.

The Board shall, moreover, in presenting its suggestions and recommendations relating to the several institutions under its supervision, and also as to the general interests of insane persons throughout the State, present information embodying the experience of institutions for the insane in this and other countries, regarding the best and most successful methods of caring for the insane; and it shall also encourage scientific investigation in the matter and treatment of insanity by the medical staffs of the various institutions, and shall publish from time to time bulletins and reports of the scientific and clinical work done therein.

The Board shall further inspect all plans for new buildings, and for the extension, alteration or repair of existing buildings, to be used by the State as hospitals or asylums for the insane, and no such building or extension or addition shall be hereafter constructed for that purpose unless the plan for its construction is first approved by the Board.

The Board shall keep records of patients and attend to the enforcement of the laws in regard to commitments, and keep records of the same; and all institutions under its inspection and supervision shall be obliged to furnish all the information required by the Board.

State Care of the Insane.

We recommend that all insane persons, acute and chronic, who are supported at public expense, be placed under the care, custody and control of the authorities of the Commonwealth, and that the expense of their support be borne entirely by the Commonwealth. This, we are aware, is a somewhat radical change from the existing system, but we believe that it is for the interest of the insane within the Commonwealth to have it carried out.

The principal reasons which have led us to make this recommendation are: first, that the treatment of the insane would be uniform; second, that such treatment would in all cases be under the direction of the best and most advanced expert knowledge attainable in the Commonwealth, and thus in some instances more humane; third, that the application of the settlement laws to insane paupers would be seldom required; and, fourth, that economical methods in the care of the insane would be eventually more easily attained.

The tendency of the present time among the cities and towns of the Commonwealth is to remove the insane people who have a settlement within them from the care of the State authorities as soon as the acute stage of insanity has passed; in other words, when the patient becomes chronically insane and harmless, as they are in many instances, the city or town which has to pay for his or her support removes such patient from the State institution and places him or her in its almshouse, or in such institution as it may have provided for the care of the insane. The motive for this removal is that the city or town can ordinarily support a harmless chronic insane person for a less sum of money than it has to pay the State for his or her support. Moreover, it sometimes occurs that the cities and towns postpone sending their insane poor to the State institutions in the acute stages of the disease until the period in which the chances of cure are the most promising has passed.

Eight of the cities of the Commonwealth have hospitals or other receptacles for the insane in connection with their almshouses where the chronic patients are cared for, and the fact that they are in a place set apart for the insane is evidence that they are separated from the sane poor. It is, however, different, and in some cases necessarily so, in many cities and towns of the Commonwealth, where the chronic insane are placed in the almshouses, often directly among the sane poor, without any attempt to keep the two classes separate. Such a mingling of sane and insane persons leads often to unfortunate results, and we know of no better method to avoid this difficulty than that which we recommend above.

This transfer of the care and support of the insane poor to the Commonwealth will necessitate the providing by the Commonwealth of accommodations for those insane persons who are now taken care of locally in the different cities and towns, and who number approximately thirteen hundred. This number, we understand, practically represents all the insane poor for whom accommodation will have to be found by the Commonwealth. We would suggest that it might be found expedient for the Commonwealth to take possession of some of the buildings erected by the different cities for the care of their insane, as for instance, in the city of Boston. The exact method to be pursued, however, in the care of the insane poor, whom we now recommend be transferred to the care and support of the Commonwealth, can be safely left to the State Board of Insanity, if it be created as we recommend, inasmuch as the demands for the future accommodation and treatment of the insane will be more clearly seen by them than can be now anticipated by us. Some of the chronic insane can perhaps be cared for in the localities to which they belong.

We are of course aware that the adoption of the above recommendation will involve the Commonwealth in some additional expenditure of money at the outset for the construction or the taking of the buildings necessary to accommodate the increased number of insane, and also annually for their support. It is difficult to estimate the expense thus involved, but it will not be larger than the Commonwealth can properly assume, in order to carry out a reform which will be of incalculable benefit to a large class of its wards. Moreover, it is to be borne in mind that, although an additional burden would be thrown upon the Commonwealth, and through it upon the taxpayer, still, the cities and towns would be relieved of all obligation to support their insane poor, and would in this manner not only save the amounts which they expend in determining questions of settlement and in the care of those who are locally supported, but also the amounts which they have annually to pay the Commonwealth for those who are supported by it.

COMMITMENTS.

The law of the Commonwealth provides that, except when otherwise specially provided, no person shall be committed to a lunatic hospital, asylum or other receptacle for the insane, public or private, without an order or certificate therefor, signed by a judge of the supreme judicial court or superior court in any county where he may be, or a judge of the probate court or of a police, district or municipal court within his county. The order or certificate shall state that the judge finds that the person committed is insane, and is a fit person for treatment in an insane asylum; and that he either has a legal settlement in the State, or has been an inhabitant thereof for the six months immediately preceding such finding, or that arrangements satisfactory to the State Board of Lunacy and Charity have been made for his maintenance, or that, by reason of insanity, he would be dangerous if at large. The judge shall see and examine the person alleged to be insane, or state in his final order the reason why it was not deemed necessary or advisable to do so. The hearing, except when a jury is summoned, shall be at such place as the judge shall appoint. In all cases the judge shall certify in what place the lunatic resided at the time of his commitment; or, if commitment is ordered by a court, the judge shall certify at what place the lunatic resided at the time of his arrest, in pursuance of which he was held to answer before such court.

No person shall be committed unless, in addition to the oral testimony, there has been filed with the judge who hears the complaint or other proceeding for the commitment of the person alleged to be insane the certificate of two physicians, certifying to such person's insanity. The law further provides that no one shall be qualified as a physician to make to a judge the above certificate unless he shall make oath that he is a graduate of a legally chartered school or college, and that he has been in the actual practice of his profession in this Commonwealth as a physician for at least three years since graduation, and for the three years next preceding his making said oath; nor unless he is duly registered, in compliance with the provisions of chapter 458 of the Acts of the year 1894, and continues to be so registered; nor unless his standing, character and professional knowledge of insanity are satisfactory to the judge. A certificate bearing date more than ten days prior to any commitment of any person alleged to be insane shall be null and void, and no certificate shall be valid or received in evidence if signed by any physician holding any office or appointment in or connected with the hospital, asylum or other place for the insane to which the person in question may be committed by order of the judge. Every physician certifying must himself have examined the person alleged to have been insane within five days of his signing the certificate, and shall state in the certificate that in his opinion the person is insane, and a proper subject for treatment in an insane hospital or asylum, and shall certify the facts upon which his information is founded. A copy of the certificate, attested by the judge, shall be delivered by the officer or other person making the commitment to the superintendent of the hospital or other place to which the person shall be committed, and shall be filed and kept with the order of commitment. A copy of each physician's certificate of insanity shall be mailed to the State Board of Lunacy and Charity by the superintendent of each lunatic hospital and asylum within forty-eight hours after the commitment of each person adjudged to be insane.

A person applying for the commitment or for the admission of a patient to a State lunatic hospital, or to the Hospital for Dipsomaniacs and Inebriates, shall first give notice in writing to the overseers of the poor in the place where the lunatic or dipsomaniac resides, except in Boston, where the notice shall be given to the Institutions Commissioner, of his intention to make such application; and satisfactory evidence that such notice has been given shall be produced to the justice in the cases of commitment.

Upon every application for the commitment or admission of an insane person to a hospital or asylum for the insane, there shall be filed with the application, or within ten days after the commitment or admission, a statement in respect to such person showing, as nearly as can be ascertained, his age, birthplace, civil condition and occupation, the supposed cause and the duration and character of his disease, etc.; and this statement, or a copy thereof, shall be transmitted to the superintendent of the hospital or asylum, to be filed with the order of commitment or the application for admission. The superintendent shall, within two days from the time of the admission or commitment of an insane person, send or cause to be sent notice of said commitment in writing by mail, postage prepaid, to each of the relatives of the insane person that are named in the statement, or to any other two persons whom the person committed shall designate.

The law further provides that the judge may in his discretion issue a warrant to the sheriff or his deputy, directing him to summon a jury of six lawful men to hear and determine whether the alleged lunatic is insane.

Each judge is required to keep a docket or record of the causes relating to lunatics coming before him, numbered or otherwise properly designated, and the disposition of them. He shall also receive and keep on file the original application, statement of applicant, and certificate of physicians and the copy of the order of commitment, attested by and regularly returned by the officer or other person serving the same.

The superintendent or keeper of any lunatic hospital in this State, and of any city asylum for the care and treatment of the chronic insane, may receive into his custody and detain at such hospital or asylum, for any period not exceeding five days, without any order of a judge or justice, any person as insane whose case is duly certified to be one of violent and dangerous insanity and emergency, by two physicians qualified as provided by law. In addition to such certificates, an application signed by one of the selectmen of the town, or by the mayor or one of the aldermen of the city, in which said insane person resides or is found, shall be left with the superintendent of the hospital or asylum in which the insane person is received; and such application shall contain the statement in respect to such insane person which is now required by law, and a further statement that the case is one of violent and dangerous insanity.

When a patient is received into any lunatic hospital or asylum upon his own application, or as an emergency patient, the superintendent shall give immediate notice of such reception to the State Board of Lunacy and Charity, stating all the particulars in the case, including the legal settlement of the person so received, if known; and said Board shall immediately cause such cases to be investigated, and a record to be made of all the facts pertaining thereto.

Any physician who wilfully and intentionally conspires with any person, unlawfully or improperly to commit to any lunatic hospital or asylum in this State any person who is not insane, shall be punished by fine or imprisonment, at the discretion of the court.

Provision is also made for the reception by lunatic hospitals or asylums for the insane, as a boarder or patient, of any person who desires to submit himself to treatment, but whose mental condition is not such as to render it legal to grant a certificate of insanity.

Several changes and additions have been suggested to us in the course of our investigation into the law of commitments; but, in view of the facts that the laws regulating this subject have been amended within the last few years, and that they appear to be working well, we are not prepared to recommend any additional changes. We would, however, suggest that the simplification of the form of certificates now required might be obtained by providing that the Board of Insanity, if created, should prescribe a form which should be universally adopted.

Boarded-out Insane.

The State Board of Health, Lunacy and Charity was authorized in 1885 (St. 1885, c. 385) "to place at board, where they may deem it expedient, and in suitable families throughout the Commonwealth, insane persons of the chronic and quiet class, and the cost of boarding such insane persons having no settlement in this Commonwealth shall be paid from the appropriation for the support of State paupers in lunatic hospitals." Bills for the support of insane persons so boarded in families at the expense of the State were audited by the Board, and it was made the duty of the Board to cause all insane persons who were so boarded in families to be visited at least once in three months; and all insane persons who were boarded in families at the expense of towns and cities and whose residence was made known to the Board, to be visited at least once in six months by some agent of the Board. The Board was also required to remove to a lunatic hospital or to some better boarding-place all State paupers who upon visitation were found to be abused, neglected or improperly cared for, when boarded out, and might also remove to a lunatic hospital any insane person boarded at the expense of a city or town who should be found unsuitably provided with a boarding-place. In 1886 (St. 1886, c. 101, § 4) the above authority was vested in the State Board of Lunacy and Charity.

As previously stated, the number of boarded-out insane under the above provision of the statutes, on Sept. 30, 1895, according to the report of the State Board of Lunacy and Charity for the year 1895, was 142. Although we believe that this authority can remain with the State Board of Insanity, if created according to our recommendations, until the number of insane persons boarded out reaches such proportions that a separate department should be created to take charge of the work, we see no reason why the boards of trustees of the several hospitals and asylums for the insane should not also have the power to board out insane persons of the character described who are in the institutions under their control, as well as the State Board of Insanity. The work of the boards of trustees in this regard should be of course subject to the supervision of the State Board of Insanity. We therefore recommend that the law be changed so as to carry out the above recommendation.

General Suggestions.

Great weight should be attached to the thorough inspection of all the hospitals and asylums for the insane brought under the supervision of the State Board of Insanity, and in order to insure such inspection we would suggest that the following provisions be incorporated in the law and made mandatory: —

First. — That the Board or any two members of it should visit every hospital and asylum under its supervision at least twice a year.

Second. — That every part of the institution visited should be carefully inspected.

Third. — That every patient should be interviewed, or an opportunity offered to each one to hold an interview.

Fourth. — That every certificate of commitment entered or filed since the last visitation should be inspected.

Fifth. — That entries should be made by the visiting Board or the visiting members in a visitors' book of minutes of the condition of the institution at that time, of the patients therein, of the patients under restraint and their number, and any criticisms or observations that the Board or visiting members may have to make, — for instance, as to the occupation, amusement or classification of the patients, as to the cleanliness and sanitary condition of the institution, as to the diet of the patients, and any other matters that they may deem worthy of observation or criticism.

We further recommend: —

That all patients in any hospital, asylum or receptacle for the insane shall be allowed, subject to the regulations of the Board, to write freely to the State Board of Insanity, if created, and that the letters so written shall be forwarded unopened by the superintendent or person in charge to the said Board, for such disposition as it shall deem right; and that the said Board shall have the right to send any letters, or other communications that it may deem proper, to such patients.

That whenever any person is received by the superintendent or physician in charge of any insane hospital or asylum, and there is a question as to the propriety of his or her commitment, the said superintendent or physician shall immediately notify the State Board of Insanity, who shall inquire into the insanity of such patient and into the question of the propriety of the commitment.

That, in taking and transferring patients to and from the

institutions for the insane, the nurses of the hospitals and asylums should be employed, as far as practicable, instead of officers of the law.

That a uniform system of keeping accounts in the several State hospitals and asylums be prescribed by the State Board of Insanity, and that the same be universally adopted by those institutions.

That the State Board of Insanity and the boards of trustees of the several hospitals and asylums for the insane, whose responsibilities should not be lessened, meet quarterly for purposes of consultation and harmonious action. Some of the topics to be considered at such meetings might be the apportionment of patients to the several hospitals and asylums, the examination by experts of questions of diet, ventilation, drainage, new construction, improved facilities for treating acute curable cases, occupation for the patients and gymnastics as a means of physical and mental training.

That there be referred to the Board or its officers questions of the sanity of inmates of the penal, reformatory and other institutions who present indications of insanity.

That the use of the word "lunatic" be abandoned, and that the term "insane" or "insane person" be substituted for it wherever it occurs in the names of the several hospitals and in the laws relating to the insane.

We submit a bill, incorporating the above recommendations, in Appendix B.

LAWS OF SETTLEMENT.

Every pauper within the confines of the State of Massachusetts is supported in one of two ways, either by the city or town in which he has a settlement, or by the Commonwealth if he has no settlement. If he has no settlement, the question of his support is a simple one. If, however, he has a settlement, the further question arises, in what city or town he has that settlement. The determination of the questions whether a pauper has or has not a settlement, and where his settlement is if he has one, calls for the application of the settlement laws of the Commonwealth. Through the application of these laws is determined the proportion of the expenditure for the support of the paupers found within the State that the Commonwealth and the cities and towns shall severally bear.

In another part of this report we have recommended that all insane paupers be supported by the Commonwealth. The result of this recommendation, if adopted, will be to relieve the cities and towns from any obligation to support insane paupers having settlements therein, and to this extent questions arising under the settlement laws will be diminished in number. Thereafter they will arise mainly in regard to the support of sane paupers.

Various suggestions have been presented to us, looking to a change in the settlement laws as they at present exist. These suggestions were presented by persons who have had the largest experience in the administration of these laws within the Commonwealth. All the changes which we recommend, with some slight exceptions, are changes which have been approved by the Massachusetts Association of Relief Officers, which is an association composed of many of the overseers of the poor of different cities and towns of the Commonwealth and their executive officers; and most of them are approved by the agent of the present Board of Lunacy and Charity, who has special charge of the administration of the settlement laws on the part of the Commonwealth.

In concluding to recommend the changes which we present below, we have had constantly in mind a consideration which we believe to be most important for the welfare of the poor who are dependent upon public charity in the Commonwealth; namely, that they should be kept, as far as possible, out of institutions, and should be supported in the different localities to which they belong. The reasons which have brought us to recommend that the insane poor should be supported and cared for by the Commonwealth might, in some of their aspects, also lead us to recommend consistently that the Commonwealth take charge of all the poor dependent upon public charity, sane as well as insane, and pay for their maintenance and support. We are not, however, prepared to approve so radical a change as this in the existing system of support of the dependent poor within the Commonwealth. The demand, moreover, for uniform and expert treatment which forms so large a consideration in dealing with the insane poor, does not apply with equal force to the care and support of the sane. If, however, at any time hereafter, it should be deemed proper to make this change, we have no doubt that the advisability of the Commonwealth supporting the poor dependent upon public charity in the different cities and towns where they belong will be recognized, and that the placing of the poor, of which it has the care and support, in institutions will be carefully limited. However this may be, we believe, at the present time, that it is better that the existing system of local support should continue, so far as the sane poor are concerned; and, while this is so, we believe that the prerequisites to obtaining a settlement should be made lighter than they are at present, and that in some other respects the laws of settlement should be simplified and made clearer. We therefore recommend: —

First. — That all settlements acquired by virtue of any provision of law in force prior to the passage of the act approved May 13, 1865, entitled "An act relating to the settlement and relief of persons who have served in the army and navy of the United States," should be defeated and lost, except where the existence of such settlement prevented a subsequent acquisition of settlement in the same place; provided, that whenever a settlement acquired by marriage has been thus defeated, the former settlement of the wife, if not defeated by the same provision, shall be thereby revived.

No settlements have been lost in Massachusetts since 1794, (see St. 1870, chap. 392, § 2; St. 1878, chap. 190, § 4) and it seems proper to fix a later period within which they shall be lost. The year 1865 has been fixed upon, because at that time there was much legislation in favor of the soldier and the sailor, and it is deemed inadvisable to affect in any way whatever rights they may have obtained under that legislation.

Second. — That legitimate children, until they gain a settlement of their own, shall follow and have the settlement of their parents or surviving parent, or of the parent to whom the children are awarded in case of divorce, if the parents or parent have any within the State.

The law at present provides that legitimate children shall follow and have the settlement of the father if he has any within the State, until they gain a settlement of their own; but if he has none, they shall in like manner follow and have the settlement of the mother if she has any. The reason for this suggested change is, that under the present law the surviving parent and the children are sometimes separated in their support. For instance, a man and a woman marry; they have a child; the husband who has a settlement dies; the wife marries a second husband, who has a settlement in some other part of the State, and she of course takes the settlement. If they fall into distress, the mother and child are separated; the child's settlement may be in one place, and the mother's in another. The result of the change suggested would be, that children would follow the settlement of the surviving parent, so that, if the surviving parent becomes dependent upon public charity, such parent and the children will be helped by the same community and in the same way. The suggestion as to the disposition of children in case of divorce is made for the same reason.

Third. — That any person of the age of twenty-one years who resides in any place within this State for three years together shall thereby gain a settlement in such place.

The law at present provides that any person of the age of twenty-one years who resides in any place within the State for five years together, and pays all State, county, city or town taxes duly assessed on his poll or estate for any three years within that time, shall thereby gain a settlement in such place; and that any woman of the age of twenty-one years who resides in any place within the State for five years together shall thereby gain a settlement in such place. Before 1874 the law required a residence of ten years and the payment of taxes for five years. Following the policy of the legislature in 1874, we believe that the number of years residence should be reduced to three and that the payment of taxes as a prerequisite to obtaining a settlement be done away with. The poll tax as a prerequisite for voting has been abolished, and the class of people who are likely to fall into distress will not probably pay any more poll taxes; so it seems that the result of retaining the provision requiring payment of a tax as a prerequisite to acquiring a settlement would be that people of the class that are likely to be most in need of assistance will never become settled. Men and women, moreover, if the above changes are adopted, will be placed on exactly the same footing, so far as the acquisition of a settlement is concerned.

Fourth. — No person shall be in process of acquiring a settlement while receiving relief as a pauper, unless within three years from the time of receiving such relief the city or town is reimbursed the cost thereof.

The object of this provision is, of course, apparent; and the provision itself corresponds exactly with the present law, excepting as to the number of years within which the city or town furnishing the relief must be reimbursed the cost thereof. The present law fixes that number at five years. The recommendation above changes the time from five years to three, so that this provision of law will be in accordance with the time of residence recommended above as a prerequisite for the acquisition of a settlement.

Fifth. — That all persons absent from the Commonwealth for ten years in succession shall lose their settlements.

This would be a new provision of law in this Commonwealth. In the State of Maine settlements are lost by living five consecutive years beyond the limits of the State, and in New Hampshire all settlements acquired before 1880 are defeated. We believe that a person who lives out of the State for ten years continuously should not be allowed, when in need of public aid, to return to this State and claim a settlement in a city or town in which he had not resided for so many years.

Sixth. — That no person who has begun to acquire a settlement by the laws in force at or before the time the above changes are made shall be prevented or delayed by these provisions, but shall acquire a settlement in the same time and in the same manner as if the former laws had continued in force.

We recommend that the above changes should not take effect until January 1, 1898, in order to give the cities and towns of the Commonwealth an opportunity to adapt themselves to the new law.

We submit a bill incorporating the above recommendations in Appendix C.

HOSPITAL FOR DIPSOMANIACS AND INEBRIATES.

The statute of 1885, chapter 329, was the first attempt in the legislation of this Commonwealth to provide for the treatment of dipsomania or habitual drunkenness as a disease. That act authorized the committal of a person subject to dipsomania or habitual drunkenness, whether in public or in private, to one of the State Lunatic Hospitals, when such a person was not of bad repute or of bad character, apart from his habits of inebriety. It was found from experience that the commitment of such persons to State lunatic hospitals was subject to difficulties, and in 1889 there was passed an act to establish the Massachusetts Hospital for Dipsomaniacs and Inebriates (St. 1889, chapter 414). The hospital authorized by the above legislation was opened in 1893, and has been in existence, therefore, a little over three years.

We understand that the objects of the creation of this hospital were to treat inebriety or drunkenness in a scientific manner as a disease, to enable persons supposed to be suffering from this disease to be committed to the hospital without the stigma attaching to them consequent upon a committal to a penal or reformatory institution, and to relieve the insane hospitals.

The fact must be recognized that in establishing this institution the Commonwealth undertook a novel experiment, the value of which cannot be determined immediately. The statistics showing the results of the work of the hospital looking towards the permanent improvement of the persons committed thereto are naturally meagre, and it would be premature to judge of the future by the results of the work of the institution at the present time.

There has been recently a reorganization of the Board of Trustees, and although, so far as information can be obtained, the full purpose for which the hospital was created has not yet been attained, still, we feel that the experiment of the maintenance of such an institution has hardly as yet received a fair test. If the experiment be worth undertaking at all, it seems that the Commonwealth should deal generously with the institution.

In order to better effect the original objects of the hospital, and to render the experiment more satisfactory, we recommend the following changes in the legislation which already governs the institution: —

First. — That the Board of Trustees of the hospital shall have authority at any time, when a patient has been long enough in the hospital to enable it to form an opinion as to whether or not the treatment will benefit him, to finally discharge such patient.

Second. — That the State Board of Insanity shall have the same powers in regard to this institution that it will have in regard to insane hospitals, if the transfer of authority recommended to be made in this report is perfected. These will include the power to discharge patients from the hospital and to transfer the inmates of the hospital to other State institutions and the inmates of the other State institutions to the hospital.

Third. — That the State Board of Insanity shall prescribe the forms for commitment to the hospital, and that forms so prescribed shall be universally used in the commitment of patients.

Fourth. — That a system be devised by the State Board of Insanity by which the Board of Trustees of the hospital shall be informed more specifically of the history of the patient at the time of commitment, and by which, if possible, an investigation of the record of the patient should be made by a probation officer with the view of informing the judge prior to his taking action upon the question of commitment.

We submit a bill incorporating the above recommendations in Appendix D.

STATE BOARD OF CHARITY.

If the recommendations that we have suggested above for the creation of a State Board of Insanity and a Department for Children be adopted, we recommend that a State Board of Charity be created, to which shall be given all the powers and duties which would have remained to the present State Board of Lunacy and Charity, if continued, after withdrawing from that Board the powers and duties given respectively to the State Board of Insanity and to the Department for Children.

We recommend that this Board be composed of seven members, who shall each hold office for seven years. They shall be appointed by the governor, by and with the consent and advice of the council, and one of them shall be designated by the governor as secretary of the Board, and shall receive a salary of $3,500 and his actual expenses. The other members of the Board shall receive no compensation except their expenses actually incurred in the performance of their duties.

The Board shall have power to appoint such agents and other subordinate officers as may be necessary, and to fix their compensation, subject to the approval of the Governor and Council.

By the transfer of the powers above referred to, there would descend to the State Board of Charity from the present State Board of Lunacy and Charity, the general supervision of the sane paupers at the State Almshouse and State Farm, the Lyman School for Boys and the Industrial School for Girls; and it would be required to visit, by its agents, those institutions at least as often as once in each month. We recommend, however, in another part of this report, that the State Farm be eventually used solely for prisoners sentenced by the courts, and that when this arrangement is perfected it be placed under the supervision of the Commissioners of Prisons.

The Board would be required to present a review of the work of the several institutions under its supervision for the preceding year, with such suggestions relating to them and to the general charitable interests of the State as may be deemed expedient. It would be required to report annually a properly classified and tabulated statement of the receipts and expenses of all institutions under its supervision; a corresponding classified and tabulated statement of its estimates for the year ensuing, and as to the necessity or expediency of appropriations in accordance with the estimates.

It would prescribe the forms for the statistical returns required by law to be made by the superintendents of the State institutions, and by the mayors of cities or the overseers of the poor of towns. It would prepare, from returns made by the overseers of the poor, the tables of sane paupers supported by towns.

It would be obliged to visit, at least once in every year, all places where State sane paupers are supported, and ascertain from actual examination and inquiry whether the laws in regard to such paupers are properly observed, particularly in relation to those who are able to labor, and to give such directions as will insure correctness in the returns required in relation to paupers. It would have the same powers relating to State sane paupers who are inmates of the State Almshouse and to their property as are vested in towns and overseers of the poor in reference to paupers supported or relieved by towns.

It would administer the laws relating to cases of persons,

liable to be maintained by the Commonwealth, who are infected with diseases dangerous to the public health or whose health would be endangered by removal to the State Almshouse.

It would administer the laws relating to cases of poor and indigent persons where the wife has a legal settlement and the husband is a State pauper, and the laws relating to cases of temporary aid to poor persons having no lawful settlement within the Commonwealth.

It would have the power to transfer sane pauper inmates from one State institution to another, or to send such paupers to any State or place where they belong. Upon an application of the trustees of the Lyman and Industrial Schools, it could transfer inmates of the schools to the State Farm or return them to the schools; and it could, in certain cases, transfer inmates of the State Almshouse to the State Farm.

It would have the determination of questions relating to the settlement or non-settlement of State sane paupers coming under the control of the State institutions under its supervision, the general administration of the laws of settlement relating to the support of State sane paupers by cities and towns, and the prosecution of cases of bastardy of non-settled persons.

We recommend, in addition to the powers and duties above outlined, and which, as we have said, would descend to the State Board of Charity, if created, from the present State Board of Lunacy and Charity:

That the State Board of Charity should have charge of the interests of the Commonwealth upon the subject of charity generally, and should investigate the causes of pauperism and existing and proposed methods and practices in the administration of relief of the poor.

That the Board should publish from time to time information on the work of public and private charitable agencies in other States and countries, so far as the same may be deemed applicable to the needs of this Commonwealth; that it should publish, periodically or otherwise, bulletins to be distributed to public officials and to other persons, and should establish a bureau of information for persons engaged or interested in public or private charities.

That the Board should have the general supervision of the Department for Children, if created, the county and municipal reformatories and homes for children, city and town almshouses, tramp houses and receptacles for tramps or vagrants.

That all plans or estimates for new sites and new buildings, for the extension, alteration or repair of existing buildings, for the arrangement of grounds or systems of sewerage, or for heating with reference to buildings which are, or will be when completed, subject to the visitation of the Board, should, before adoption, be submitted to the Board for its advice and suggestion.

That the Board should promote measures designed to secure a uniform policy in the treatment of tramps and vagrants throughout the Commonwealth.

Questions will arise as to the settlement of the insane poor and of certain other persons to the extent of determining whether or not they should be supported by the Commonwealth or removed to the State in which they have a settlement. We, therefore, recommend, in order to avoid the establishment by the State Board of Insanity of a separate department for the determination of such matters, that questions of the nature above described be referred to the State Board of Charity, to be determined by such department as the latter Board may establish to pass upon the settlement cases arising in regard to the sane poor.

The powers and duties above described are sufficient to occupy the entire attention of a Board such as we suggest to be created.

In connection with the general subject of the supervision of public charitable institutions, the value of voluntary local visitation should be recognized. Our attention has been directed to the work of the State Charities Aid Association in New York. Good can doubtless be accomplished in this Commonwealth by the development of work of this nature in the visitation of almshouses and municipal homes for children.

The most satisfactory results in dealing with the poor, both adult and children, can be reached by enlisting the intelligence and activity of a number of persons of varied and broad experience in dealing with problems of charity and education. We call attention with approval to the practice in a few cities and towns of the Commonwealth of electing women to the boards of overseers of the poor; and in general we recommend that charitable institutions be governed by boards rather than by individuals.

We submit a bill incorporating the above recommendations in Appendix E.

REFORMATORY AND PENAL INSTITUTIONS.

The reformatory and penal institutions of the Commonwealth consist of the State Prison, the Massachusetts Reformatory at Concord and the Reformatory Prison for Women at Sherborn. These three institutions are under the control of and are maintained and supported entirely by the Commonwealth. They are subject to the supervision of the Commissioners of Prisons. In addition there is the State Farm at Bridgewater, subject to the supervision of the State Board of Lunacy and Charity.

According to the report of the warden of the State Prison, submitted to the Legislature in January, 1896, in the report of the Commissioners of Prisons, there were 700 convicts in the State Prison on September 30, 1895. According to the report of the superintendent of the Reformatory Prison for Women, submitted at the same time, there were, on the latter date, 336 in the custody of that reformatory. By the report of the superintendent of the Massachusetts Reformatory, there were on the same date 1,011 inmates of that reformatory, making in all 2,047 in the custody of the above-named institutions at the time named.

There were during the year ending September 30, 1895, 172 commitments to the State Prison, 334 to the Reformatory Prison for Women and 774 to the Massachusetts Reformatory, making in all 1,280 persons committed by the courts during the year to the above institutions.

Besides the institutions above named, there are twenty-two county jails and county houses of correction, including those in the city of Boston. Five of the above are jails, which are used mainly for the detention of persons awaiting trial; three are houses of correction used exclusively for sentenced prisoners, and fourteen of them consist of a jail and house of correction under the same roof and management. These jails and houses of correction are subject to the supervision of the Commissioners of Prisons, but they are supported and maintained by the several counties, the officer in charge of the jails in every case being the sheriff of the county, and the officer in charge of the houses of correction, excepting in the city of Boston, being also the sheriff or a superintendent or master appointed by him. In the city of Boston, the House of Industry, now called the House of Correction at Deer Island (St. 1896, c. 536), and the House of Correction at South Boston are each in the charge of a master appointed by the Institutions Commissioner. The control of all the supplies for these county institutions, except in the county of Suffolk, is in the hands of the county commissioners of the several counties. The county commissioners have, moreover, a general oversight of the administration of the institutions. In the county of Suffolk the Institutions Commissioner performs in this regard the functions of county commissioners in other counties.

The Commissioners of Prisons, moreover, have the power to make rules for the government of these institutions, and those rules take precedence of all others.

On September 30, 1895, there were 2,240 prisoners in the House of Industry in the city of Boston, now called the House of Correction at Deer Island, and in the House of Correction at South Boston, and 2,767 in the other county prisons, making a total of 5,007 inmates of the county jails and houses of correction at the time named, and making a total, including those in the custody of the State institutions and the State Farm, of 7,628 prisoners.

There were during the year ending September 30, 1895, 8,458 commitments to the House of Industry and 16,665 commitments to the other county jails and houses of correction, making a total of 25,123 commitments to the House of Industry and to the other county jails and houses of correction during the time named, to which if we add the commitments made during the year to the State Prison, the Reformatory Prison for Women and the Massachusetts Reformatory, we have a total of 26,403 prisoners, who have during the year been committed to all the prisons above named. To these should be added 1,063 prisoners who were committed during the year to the State Farm.

The County Jails and Houses of Correction.

The statute of 1870, c. 370, entitled "An Act for the appointment of Commissioners of Prisons, and for the classification and better discipline of prisoners," provided in section 2 that the commissioners should "as far as practicable classify all prisoners held under sentence in all jails and houses of correction in the State, or that may be committed thereto at any time hereafter, having reference to sex, age, character, condition and offences, and in such manner as to promote the reformation, safe custody and economy of support of the prisoners, and of the separation of male and female prisoners; and for this purpose they may remove prisoners from one jail to another jail in the same or in any other county, and from one house of correction to another in the same or in any other county, and the said prisoners shall serve the remainder of their terms of sentence in the prisons to which they shall be so removed from time to time."

It further provided, in section 4, that the courts "may sentence any person convicted before such court of an offence punishable by imprisonment in the jail or house of correction to any jail or house of correction of any county in the Commonwealth. And the jailer, or master, or keeper of the house of correction or jail to which such person shall be sentenced, or to which any person may be removed under this act, shall receive and detain such person or prisoner in the same manner as if committed by any court sitting in the county where said jail or house of correction is situated."

These provisions of law have remained unchanged up to the present time. The classification above described has been found to be impracticable for several reasons. The county in which a prisoner was sentenced objected to paying for his support and maintenance in another county, feeling that it could support its prisoners within its own limits cheaper than they could be supported outside. The opinion also prevails among the county authorities that persons convicted of offences within the county are in many instances best dealt with locally. The fact, moreover, that the Commonwealth has not the entire control of the prisons in question renders it impossible to set apart particular prisons for specific uses. For these reasons among others, the attempt to bring about a classification such as that contemplated by the above statute has been abandoned, so that now there is no progressive classification in the county prisons.

The policy which led the Legislature of the Commonwealth to enact the above provisions of law, and which led the Legislature more recently to create, in 1874, the Reformatory Prison for Women, and, in 1884, the Massachusetts Reformatory for the younger male prisoners, will, if pursued, undoubtedly in time lead to the placing of all the prisoners who are now sent to the county jails and houses of correction under the direct care and control of the authorities of the Commonwealth. The two institutions above named were established because it was felt at the time of their creation that some further effort should be made to classify the different criminals within the Commonwealth, and to give those who were young in years an opportunity at least to reform, if they were capable of reformation. There was a strong realization at that time and earlier that the massing of the young and old criminals, the comparatively innocent with the most depraved, resulted in an increase of crime. The women who were susceptible of reform were, therefore, sent to Sherborn, and the younger men, between fifteen and thirty-five years of age, who were deemed susceptible of reformatory treatment, were taken to

Concord. The want of classification and of opportunities for reformation so strongly felt twenty-five years ago is even more fully apparent at the present time.

The number of commitments to the county jails and houses of correction, according to the report of the Commissioners of Prisons above referred to, goes on increasing from year to year, and to meet this increase there is no corresponding development of reformatory measures.

It is important in this connection to note that according to the figures for the year ending September 30, 1895, there were nearly 1,300 commitments to county prisons, including the Boston House of Industry, of persons who were under twenty-one years of age, including 280 under eighteen, and 9,163 others were of persons between twenty-one and thirty years of age. In other words, there were more than 10,000 commitments of persons not above thirty years of age.

If we examine into the class of offences for which prisoners were committed to these institutions, we find that 961 of the 4,558 in the county prisons on the 30th of September, 1895, were held because of failure to pay fines and costs imposed for petty offences, 2,714 others were serving sentences not exceeding one year for small misdemeanors, and together with these, in close relationship with them, were 883 prisoners who had sentences from one year to five years for grave crimes against person and property. These instances are cited to show a condition of things from which evil consequences must naturally be expected to follow. It is impossible that a person who is guilty of some misdemeanor, to which he was impelled perhaps more by folly than by viciousness, should be associated for any length of time with hardened criminals and be affected in any way but for the worse. It needs no argument to show that such association must have the most disastrous effect upon a person who, if differently placed, might naturally be susceptible to reformatory treatment. There can be no doubt, also, that many men, even if not educated in a school of crime, by living lives of enforced idleness in our county prisons go out less capable of self-respect and self-support than when they were committed.

It is difficult to say, moreover, why in the nature of things there should be two classes of prisons, one supported by the Commonwealth and the other by the counties. The offences which are punished by imprisonment are all offences against the laws of the Commonwealth, and there is no reason why, of two men who are guilty of the same offence, one should be sent to a State institution and another to an institution supported by the county. There might have been some reason for the existence of county prisons in accordance with the customs of the times when the law provided that a man guilty of an offence should be sentenced to the prison of the county in which he had committed the crime, but that provision of law which had existed for many years was abrogated in 1870. (St. 1870, c. 370, sec. 4.)

STATE CONTROL OF PRISONS.

We recommend that the distinction between county prisons and prisons under the control of the State be done away with, and that all of the prisons within the Commonwealth be placed under the sole control of and be maintained by the Commonwealth. By such change the following results may be attained: —

1. The abolition of unclassified prisons.
2. The initiation and development of reformatory measures for a larger number of prisoners who are susceptible to reform.
3. Uniformity in the management of the prisons and the prisoners.
4. Uniformity in the terms of sentences and in the granting of permits to be at liberty.
5. The better regulation of labor in the prisons.
6. The more complete separation of the sexes.
7. The abandonment of prisons now quite unfit for their purpose, as, for instance, the House of Correction at South Boston, and wiser provisions for relieving our overcrowded prisons.
8. The more intelligent study and treatment of the problem of drunkenness.

We recommend that a superintendent for each of the prisons which may be provided by the Commonwealth for the prisoners who are now sentenced to the county prisons be appointed by the Governór, by and with the advice and consent of the council, upon the nomination of the Commissioners of Prisons, if organized as recommended below; that each superintendent shall have the power to appoint all his subordinate officers and to fix their compensation, subject to the approval of the Commissioners of Prisons, and that such subordinate officers shall in each case hold their offices during the pleasure of the superintendent and the Commissioners.

That each such superintendent shall have the custody and control of all the prisoners committed to the prison under his charge, and shall have the management and direction of the prison under the rules and regulations of the same. He shall purchase all the supplies necessary for the prison, and shall receive and pay out all the money paid from the treasury of the Commonwealth for the support thereof, and shall have the custody and control of the buildings and the property of the Commonwealth connected therewith.

That the Commissioners of Prisons shall have the general supervision of each of said prisons, and shall make all necessary rules and regulations for the government and direction of the officers, for the discharge of their duties, for the discipline of prisoners and for the custody and preservation of the property of the prisons, and that they shall in other respects have and exercise the same powers over such prisons as they now or hereafter shall exercise over the other prisons belonging to the Commonwealth.

That there shall be a chaplain and a physician for each of the said prisons, each of whom shall be appointed by the Governor, by and with the advice and consent of the council, upon the nomination of the Commissioners of Prisons.

That the jails in the several counties be used for the detention of persons awaiting trial and witnesses, and that they, so far as is practicable, remain under the immediate control of the sheriffs of the several counties as they are at present.

That a certain number of sentenced prisoners may be committed to jails, with the approval of the Commissioners of Prisons.

We further recommend that the Commissioners of Prisons should be given all the powers and duties now exercised by and incumbent upon the county commissioners of the several counties relating to the release of prisoners on permits to be at liberty and otherwise. The bestowal of these powers and the throwing of the burden of these duties upon the Commissioners of Prisons will increase to a large extent the powers and duties already exercised by them. It would be too much to expect that an unpaid board of commissioners, such as the Commissioners of Prisons are at present, should be obliged to perform these laborious and important functions in addition to those which they perform at present, and we therefore recommend that two members of the Commissioners of Prisons be paid each a salary of $5,000 a year, and be required to devote their whole time to the performance of their duties as members of the commission. If two members of the Commissioners of Prisons are paid adequate salaries, the Commonwealth will have the service of two persons who can afford to devote their whole time to its service, and at the same time will secure through the unpaid members such advice and counsel as they may be able to render.

We further recommend that the Commonwealth shall have the right to purchase or take such of the land and buildings now used for the county prisons as it may be deemed best to make use of in carrying out the recommendations made above.

Accommodation for the prisoners now in the county jails and houses of correction may be furnished by the Commonwealth in such a way as may hereafter be judged advisable, by taking all the present county buildings, by taking only such as may be advantageously used, or by new construction. Questions of this nature must be decided by the authorities who have the change of system to carry out.

The adoption of the above recommendations will involve expense to the Commonwealth in the taking of land and buildings, in the payment of salaries and in the maintenance of the institutions. On the other hand the counties will be saved the expense now incumbent upon them in the maintenance of their jails and houses of correction and in the support of the criminals who are a charge upon them. There can be no doubt that the immediate expense to the Commonwealth will be amply repaid by the beneficent results to the community from this change. If the system is developed with care and skill its eventual result will be what the result of the scientific treatment and classification of criminals has been elsewhere, a less number of prisoners to be supported, and less expense to the State.

The State Farm.

According to the report of the State Board of Lunacy and Charity for 1896, there were on September 30, 1895, at this institution 574 prisoners, 244 insane criminals and 135 paupers, making a total of 953 inmates, of whom 818 were criminals, either sane or insane. It is needless to present arguments to show that the association in the same institution of sane and insane criminals and of the sane poor, dependent upon public charity, is undesirable and cannot, in the nature of things, lead to the best results.

We recommend that the insane criminals be removed from the State asylum for insane criminals at Bridgewater as soon as is practicable, and moreover, that the paupers at the State Farm, who are comparatively so few in number, be removed to some other institution or place away from the close association with criminals; that the State Farm be eventually used as one of the prisons of the Commonwealth solely for the occupation of prisoners sentenced by the courts; that it be governed in the same manner as the other prisons and be placed under the supervision of the Commissioners of Prisons.

Release of Prisoners upon Permits to be at Liberty.

The law of the Commonwealth (P. S., c. 88, § 6, c. 220, §§ 66, 68; Sts. 1884, c. 152; 1889, c. 245; 1895, c. 449, § 16) provides that when it appears to the county commissioners, or in the county of Suffolk to the Institutions Commissioner, that persons confined in a jail, house of correction or other place of confinement in their respective jurisdictions, on conviction before a trial justice or police, district or municipal court of any of the following offences, have reformed, viz.: of being rogues, vagabonds, persons who use any juggling or any unlawful games or plays, pipers and fiddlers, stubborn children, runaways, common drunkards, common night-walkers, both male and female, pilferers, lewd, wanton and lascivious persons in speech or behavior, common railers and brawlers, persons who neglect their calling or employment, misspend what they earn and do not provide for themselves or for the support of their families, and all other disorderly persons, including those persons who neglect all lawful business and habitually spend their time by frequenting houses of ill fame, gaming houses or tippling shops; or that persons imprisoned for drunkenness in a jail, house of correction or other place of confinement in their respective jurisdictions have reformed, the county commissioners and the Institutions Commissioner, the latter with the approval of a justice of the court which imposed the sentence, may issue to such persons a permit to be at liberty during the remainder of their terms of sentence; and the authority that has issued such a permit may revoke the same at any time previous to the expiration of the original terms of sentence.

If the holder of a permit shall violate any of the terms or conditions of the permit, or any laws of this Commonwealth, such violation shall of itself make the permit void; and when any permit, granted as aforesaid, has been revoked by the authority which granted it, or has become void, that authority may issue an order authorizing the arrest of the holder of the permit and his return to the place of confinement from which he was released. The holder of the permit, when returned to the place of confinement from which he was released, shall be detained therein according to the terms of his original sentence, and in computing the period of his confinement, the time between his release upon said permit and his return to said place of confinement shall not be taken to be any part of the term of his sentence.

The law gives to the State Board of Lunacy and Charity like powers of release of persons confined for like offences in the State Farm.

The county commissioners, and for the county of Suffolk the Institutions Commissioner, may release, upon such conditions as they deem best, any person imprisoned in a jail or house of correction for an offence other than a felony upon a sentence of not more than six months, or upon a longer sentence of which not more than six months remains unexpired, if a probation officer recommends the release of the prisoner and the court which imposed the sentence, or in case of the superior court, the district attorney, concurs in such recommendation. They may require a bond for the fulfilment of the conditions, and the surety upon such a bond may at any time take and surrender his principal to the county commissioners or the Institutions Commissioner, and they may at any time order such a prisoner to return to the prison from which he was released. (P. S., c. 220, § 69; Sts. 1889, c. 245; 1895, c. 449, § 16.)

After six months from the time of sentence the county commissioners or the Institutions Commissioner, the latter with the approval of a justice of the court which imposed the sentence, may discharge any person committed to the house of correction, and the directors of a workhouse or house of industry may discharge any person committed to such institution as a common night-walker upon being satisfied that the prisoner has reformed. (P. S., c. 220, § 67; Sts. 1889, c. 245; 1895, c. 449, § 16.) This power is vested in the State Board of Lunacy and Charity as to inmates of the State Farm. (P. S., c. 88, § 6; St. 1886, c. 101, § 4.)

The Commissioners of Prisons, the county commissioners, the Institutions Commissioner, the latter with the approval of a justice of the court which imposed the sentence, and the trustees of the State Farm have authority to permit prisoners to be at liberty subject to certain conditions upon deduction from the term of their imprisonment for good conduct. (P. S., c. 222, § 20; Sts. 1889, c. 245; 1894, c. 258; 1895, c. 449, § 16.)

Powers are given to the Commissioners of Prisons to issue a permit to be at liberty during the remainder of the term of sentence, upon such conditions as they deem best, to any person imprisoned in the Reformatory Prison for Women or in the Massachusetts Reformatory when it appears to the Commissioners that such person has reformed; and they may revoke such permit at any time previous to its expiration, provided that no permit shall be issued to the person transferred or removed from the State Prison to said Massachusetts Reformatory, except with the approval of the Governor and Council, and that no permit shall be issued to a person sentenced to the Reformatory Prison for Women for an offence against person or property without the consent of the court which imposed the sentence, or, in case the sentence was imposed by the superior court, without the consent of the district attorney of the county or district where said person was convicted. (P. S., c. 221, § 52; St. 1884, c. 255, § 33.)

In 1887 (St. 1887, c. 435), the Governor and Council were authorized to issue a permit to be at liberty during the remainder of his term of sentence, upon such conditions as they deem best, to any person sentenced to the State Prison as an habitual criminal when it shall appear to them that such person has reformed, and they may revoke said permit at any time previous to its expiration. The violation by the holder of a permit of any of its terms or conditions, or the violation of any of the laws of the Commonwealth, shall of itself make void said permit.

In 1894 and 1895 (Sts. 1894, c. 440, and 1895, c. 252), the Commissioners of Prisons were given the power to release any prisoner held in State Prison upon his first sentence when it shall appear to the Commissioners that he has reformed, and they may issue to him a permit to be at liberty during the remainder of his term of sentence upon such terms and conditions as they may deem best, and they may revoke said permit at any time previous to its expiration. No such permit shall be granted until at least two-thirds of his term of sentence has expired, deducting from the court sentence the time to which he may be entitled for good behavior, nor without the approval of the Governor and Council, nor unless the prisoner has an assurance satisfactory to the commissioners that he will have employment as soon as he is discharged, or is otherwise so provided for that he will not become dependent upon either public or private charity.

Upon a review of the above provisions of law, it is apparent that the only occasions when the Governor and Council are required to act in granting the permits to be at liberty are in the cases of prisoners released from the Massachusetts Reformatory who have been transferred to that institution from the State Prison, and in the cases of release of prisoners from the State Prison. It evidently was thought that when a prisoner, sentenced for a crime of such proportions as to require his imprisonment in the State Prison, was released on a permit to be at liberty, his release should have the sanction of the Governor and Council in addition to that of the Commissioners of Prisons. We see no reason why the burden of passing upon questions of this nature should be thrown upon the Governor and Council. If they are called upon to approve the action of the Commissioners of Prisons in granting permits to be at liberty, they may and do feel obliged to look into the case as thoroughly as if they were the only tribunal created to pass upon the question. This, as will be readily understood, involves much labor and great responsibility, and it seems unnecessary that two boards should be called upon to go over the same ground independently. Moreover, there seems no reason why the Commissioners of Prisons are not as capable of issuing permits to be at liberty in the cases of persons sentenced as habitual criminals as in cases of persons sentenced to the State Prison for other crimes. The issuing of permits to be at liberty would be sufficiently guarded if the power is left with the Commissioners of Prisons alone.

We therefore recommend that the provisions of law requiring original action or the approval of the Governor and

Council in the issuing of these permits, wherever they occur, be repealed, and that the Commissioners of Prisons be authorized to issue such permits in the cases of persons sentenced to the State Prison as habitual criminals.

PROBATION.

The law provides (Sts. 1891, c. 356; 1892, c. 242; 1895, c. 449, § 15) that the justices of each municipal, police or district court shall appoint one person to perform the duties of probation officer as hereinafter named under the jurisdiction of said court. The appointment of such officer for the municipal court of the city of Boston shall be made by the chief justice of said court, who may appoint as many assistants, not exceeding five, to said probation officer as are needed to carry out the purposes of the act, and each officer shall hold his office during the pleasure of the court making the appointment. Each probation officer shall inquire into the nature of every criminal case brought before the court under whose jurisdiction he acts, and may recommend that any person convicted by said court be placed upon probation, and the court may place the person so convicted in the care of said officer for such time and upon such conditions as may seem proper. Each person released upon probation shall be furnished by the probation officer with a written statement of the terms and conditions of his release, and each probation officer shall keep full records of all cases investigated by him, of all cases placed in his care by the court, and of any other duties performed by him under the law. Each probation officer, moreover, shall make a monthly report to the Commissioners of Prisons in such form as the said commissioners shall direct. The compensation of each probation officer shall be determined by the justices of the court under whose jurisdiction he acts, subject to the approval of the county commissioners of the county in which the court is located, and shall be paid from the treasury of the county upon vouchers approved by said justices and the county commissioners, or, in the county of Suffolk, by the Institutions Commissioner.

The law further provides that a probation officer may, at the request of any justice of the superior court, investigate the case of any person on trial in that court and make a report upon the same to the justice, and may upon the order of the court take on probation any person convicted in said court. The compensation for such service shall be paid from the treasury of the Commonwealth upon vouchers approved by the justice.

The probation officers may also perform the services required in the release of prisoners from the jails or houses of correction imprisoned for an offence other than felony upon a sentence of not more than six months, or upon a longer sentence of which not more than six months remain unexpired.

The chief justice of the municipal court of the city of Boston is also authorized to appoint a woman to act as assistant to the probation officer under the jurisdiction of that court, and may, subject to the approval of the Institutions Commissioner, determine her compensation, which shall be paid from the treasury of the county of Suffolk upon vouchers approved by the justice and the said commissioner. It shall be the duty of this assistant probation officer to investigate the cases of all women against whom a criminal charge is brought in said court, and to perform such duties as may be required of her by the justice of the court; and she shall hold her office during the pleasure of the chief justice. (St. 1892, c. 276.)

Actual disbursements for necessary expenses incurred by probation officers while in the performance of their duties shall be reimbursed to them out of the treasury of the county in which they serve if approved by the court or justice by whom they are appointed, provided that no officer shall be allowed for such disbursements a greater sum than one hundred dollars in any one year. (St. 1894, c. 229.) Moreover, when a person has been placed on probation, the court may authorize and direct the probation officer to expend for his or her temporary support or transportation, or for both purposes, such reasonable sum as the court shall consider expedient, and the sum so expended shall be repaid to the probation officer from the county treasury by vouchers approved by the court authorizing the expenditure. (St. 1894, c. 368.)

In case of the absence of the probation officer, the justice of any police, district or municipal court may appoint a probation officer temporarily, who shall have all the powers and perform all the duties of probation officers, and who shall receive as compensation for each day's services a sum equal to the rate per day of the salary of the probation officer, to be paid by the county; provided that the compensation so paid for in excess of every fourteen days' services by a probation officer in any one calendar year shall be deducted by the county treasurer from the salary of the probation officer. (St. 1894, c. 372.)

The above provisions of law provide for a system of probation which has worked with admirable results in this Commonwealth. The experiment of dealing with certain cases of offenders by means of probation has succeeded beyond a question, and will undoubtedly, as time goes on, be perfected in many respects as the practice of the system grows. The legislation authorizing the appointment of probation officers shows how, after the system was instituted and its value appreciated, need was felt for its extension. In 1880 the aldermen of any city, with the exception of Boston, and the selectmen of any town were authorized to establish the office of probation officer. In the city of Boston the appointment of one probation officer had been made obligatory in 1878. (P. S., c. 212, § 74, *et seq.*) In 1891 (St. 1891, c. 356) the above provisions of law were repealed and it was made mandatory upon the justice of each municipal, police or district court to appoint one probation officer, and the chief justice of the municipal court of the city of Boston was authorized to appoint assistants to the probation officer in that city not exceeding three in number. In 1892 (St. 1892, c. 242) the number of assistants which the chief justice of the municipal court of the city of Boston was authorized to appoint was increased to five.

Thus within six years the appointment of probation officers, where it was originally permissive, has been made mandatory, and the number of those officers has been largely increased in the city of Boston.

With the view of further improving the system we recommend:

That there be appointed an additional woman assistant to the probation officer of the municipal court of the city of Boston. There is need of such an assistant to properly investigate the cases of women against whom criminal charges are brought in that court.

That the chief justice of the superior court be authorized, if in his judgment it be deemed best, to appoint a probation officer for that court in the city of Boston. Many cases which would be the subjects of careful observation by the probation officer in the municipal court of the city of Boston are appealed to the superior court. We see no reason why those cases, after appeal, should not be subject to the supervision and care of a probation officer, as well as before. There are, moreover, many cases begun in the superior court which are as worthy of the attention of the probation officer as those begun in the lower courts. If, therefore, the present provision of law, authorizing a probation officer, at the request of any justice of the superior court, to investigate the case of any person on trial in that court, does not provide for ample probation service for the superior court, we deem it right that an opportunity should be given to that court to obtain a probation officer of its own, at any rate in the city of Boston.

The establishment of a Department for Children, and the adoption of the suggestions which we have made as to the necessity of having proper officers representing that department at every hearing before the courts which involve the disposition of children charged with offences, will undoubtedly aid in the careful disposition of the juvenile offenders by the different courts of the Commonwealth, and should render unnecessary the appointment of probation officers for the special supervision of children. The responsibility for work of that character should be concentrated in the Department for Children.

The special application of the system of probation to persons charged with drunkenness is dealt with in another part of this report, under the head of drunkenness.

DRUNKENNESS.

The total of the commitments to all the penal institutions for the year ending September 30, 1895, was 27,466; 18,373 of these were for drunkenness. Of the 25,123 commitments which were made in that year to the houses of correction and county jails, including the Boston House of Industry, 17,265 were for drunkenness. Of these, a number doubtless were guilty of some other offence.

From these figures we see that in each comparison the number of commitments for drunkenness is more than two-thirds of all the commitments made. Looking at it in another way, of the 336 prisoners in the custody of the Reformatory Prison for Women on September 30, 1895, 144 were in custody for drunkenness. Of the 1,011 prisoners in the Massachusetts Reformatory upon the date above mentioned, 132 were held for drunkenness. Of the 574 prisoners at the State Farm, 429 were held for drunkenness, and of the 5,007 prisoners in the county prisons, including the Boston House of Industry, 2,564 were held for drunkenness. Of 6,928 prisoners, which was the total number held in these institutions on September 30, 1895, 3,269 prisoners were in custody for drunkenness, or, in other words, almost one-half of the total number of prisoners in the prisons above named, at the time named, were held on that charge.

When one-half of the prisoners within the Commonwealth are made up of a class of people who are all convicted of one and the same offence, it seems that the time has come to direct attention particularly to the treatment of that offence, and great doubt must necessarily arise whether the best method of dealing with it has yet been discovered. Everybody must appreciate that a man who has been guilty of drunkenness alone cannot with advantage be placed in a prison to associate with men who have been guilty of crimes, and that to take a young man who has been convicted simply of being drunk and to send him to an institution with criminals will put a stamp upon him from which he may never recover.

There are many cases where a man may drink occasionally and the rest of the time be a sober, hard-working man and able to support his family. By the existing method of punishment for drunkenness by imprisonment such a man is removed from his family, is unable to support them and is placed for a greater or less period of time in the care of the State, which rarely makes any effort to reform him. In the mean while his family may be driven to become dependent upon public charity. The preservation of a man's self-respect and the proper support of his family, if he have one, receive apparently little consideration under the present method of dealing with drunkenness. The preservation of the former and the keeping, if possible, of a family from becoming dependent upon public charity are two most important constituent elements in the maintenance of a proper condition of the community, and we do not believe that a punishment which loses sight of these two most important considerations can be the right system to be employed in this Commonwealth. The Commissioners of Prisons will undoubtedly give this matter their most careful attention with a view to diminish to as great an extent as possible imprisonment as a punishment for drunkenness.

The laws regulating the punishment for drunkenness have been changed within a few years. In 1891 the provisions of law, which up to that time had governed this subject, were repealed and a new method of punishment was prescribed (St. 1891, c. 427). This method has since been changed in several respects. (See Sts. 1892, c. 303; 1893, c. 414 and c. 447.)

In 1891 punishment of drunkenness by fine was abolished, and the result was strikingly noticeable in the number of commitments for that offence. The law was approved June 11, 1891. During the year 1891 there were 19,794 commitments for drunkenness. In 1892, the year following the change in the law abolishing a fine as a penalty, there were 8,634 commitments. In 1893 the law was changed by partially restoring the fine. The St. of 1893, c. 447, provides that if a person convicted of drunkenness shall satisfy the court or trial justice by his own statement or otherwise that he has not been arrested for drunkenness twice before within twelve months next preceding, or that he has been arrested and tried twice before and acquitted in one of the cases, his case may be placed on file; or he may be punished by a fine not exceeding $15, and in case of the non-payment of such fine shall be committed to a jail, house of industry or house of correction, or to a workhouse, if there is any which has a criminal department in the city or town where the offence was committed, until the fine is paid, not, however, exceeding thirty days. The result of this change in the law was to raise the number of commitments for drunkenness in 1894 to 16,335, and since that time the number has gone on continually increasing.

The result, therefore, of the imposition of a fine as a punishment for drunkenness is to increase largely the commitments nominally for that offence to the prisons of the Commonwealth, which means that the persons committed are sent to prison, not because they have been guilty of an offence which must necessarily in itself be punished by imprisonment, but because they are too poor to pay the fine imposed upon them. Such people who are unable to raise the money to pay the fine are, in fact, imprisoned for their poverty and not for the offence of drunkenness. The result is that the man who is well off pays his fine and goes at large and the poor man is sent to prison and incurs all the disgrace attendant upon having been a criminal.

We believe that the policy declared in 1891 by the Legislature of that year, which declares against the imposition of a fine as a punishment for drunkenness, is the right policy; and we recommend that the present law be changed and that the penalty of a fine for drunkenness be abolished.

The St. of 1891, c. 427, § 6, prescribes that it shall be the duty of probation officers to assist the courts, by which they are severally appointed, by obtaining and furnishing information in regard to previous arrests, convictions and imprisonments for drunkenness, and such other facts as the court shall direct, concerning the persons accused of drunkenness. It prescribes in section seven that the probation officer shall keep a full record of each case that is investigated, and there are other provisions of the statutes, not necessary here to set out at large, providing for the full use by the courts of the records so kept.

The largest application of the probation system to the offence of drunkenness should work beneficially, both for the community and for the offenders themselves. It will likewise result in the reduction of the number of prisoners to be maintained by the Commonwealth, and thus in more economical expenditure by the Commonwealth for the care of its prisoners. If the present number of the probation officers, with the addition of a woman probation officer in the municipal court for the city of Boston, which we recommend in another part of this report, is not sufficient to furnish all the necessary information to the courts, we believe that if this fact be brought to the attention of the Legislature of the Commonwealth legislation can be secured providing for a larger number.

We recommend that if the Commonwealth assume the control and maintenance of the prisoners which are now placed in the county prisons, the indeterminate sentence law be made applicable to all persons sent to the prisons of the Commonwealth. This extension of the indeterminate sentence law will be particularly beneficial in its result when applied to prisoners convicted of drunkenness. As the law stands now, unless a person convicted of such offence is sentenced to the Massachusetts Reformatory he is sentenced to prison for a definite period, the court fixing the length of his term of sentence. The result is that, in the latter class of cases, the sentences for drunkenness differ in length of time according to the disposition of the judge, one man being sentenced perhaps for sixty days and another man for six months for the same offence. If it is provided by law that the judge shall simply sentence the offender to prison, and if the Legislature prescribes the maximum length of time during which a prisoner may be kept in prison, all persons guilty of the same offence will have similar sentences, and it will remain for the authorities having the power to release on permits to be at liberty to determine in each case whether the prisoner is fit to go at large without injury to the community and with benefit to himself and his family.

We see no reason why simple drunkenness, without other offence against the law, should be treated as a crime and be a cause of arrest, except in the case of habitual and confirmed drunkards, who should be subjected to reformatory treatment.

The resolve under which we were appointed and have pursued our investigations, and now present our recommendations, requires us to act "with a view to securing economy and efficiency in the care of the poor and insane in this Commonwealth." We are satisfied that our recommendations, if carried out, will result both in greater efficiency and in wiser economy, which includes less expense to the State.

APPENDICES.

APPENDICES.

Appendix A.

An Act to establish the department for children.

Be it enacted, etc., as follows:

Section 1. The governor, with the advice and consent of the council, shall appoint seven persons, three of whom at least shall be women, who shall constitute the department for children. The persons so appointed shall hold their offices for seven years, provided that the terms of office of the seven first appointed shall be so arranged that the term of one shall expire each year. One of the persons so appointed shall be selected from the board of trustees of the Lyman and Industrial schools. The chairman of the department shall be named by the governor, with the advice and consent of the council. All vacancies in said department, whether occurring by expiration of term or otherwise, shall be filled by the governor, with the advice and consent of the council, and no person employed by the board and receiving compensation shall be a member thereof. The members of the department may be removed by the governor, with the advice and consent of the council, for cause.

Department for children, how organized, etc.

Section 2. The department shall be a corporation for the purpose of taking, holding and investing in trust for the Commonwealth any grant or devise of lands and any gift or bequest of money or other personal property for the purposes for which it is trustee.

To be a corporation, etc.

Section 3. The department shall be provided with rooms at the expense of the state, and shall hold meetings each month on a day fixed by itself and at such other times as may be needful. It shall make its own by-laws and shall make a report of its doings to the governor and council on or before the thirty-first day of December in each year, such report being made up to the thirtieth

Meetings, report, etc.

day of September inclusive. The report shall contain a full statement of the work of the department and its expenditures, including a list of all the salaried officers employed in the department, with the salaries of said officers, and an inventory of all the property held by it as trustee for the state.

To appoint its agents, etc.

SECTION 4. The department shall have full power to appoint such agents and other subordinate officers as it deems fit, and to fix their compensation, subject to the approval of the governor and council; and the amount paid for salaries of officers and agents employed by the department shall not exceed the sum appropriated by the legislature for this purpose. The department shall have the power to make such rules and regulations governing its officers, agents and its work generally as it may deem best.

Powers, duties, etc.

SECTION 5. All the powers possessed by and all the duties incumbent upon the state board of lunacy and charity, relative to the care, custody and control of juvenile offenders and the juvenile wards of the Commonwealth, are hereby taken from the said state board of lunacy and charity and vested in the department for children, and the said department is hereby authorized and empowered to assume and exercise the same. The department shall succeed to all rights, powers and duties of the state board of lunacy and charity in regard to all juvenile offenders and juvenile wards now in charge of the state board, and the care and custody of the same are hereby transferred to said department; but this succession and transfer shall not in any way impair the sentence of any child committed to the state board of lunacy and charity, and such child shall be held by the said department under the original commitment without further process of law until the term of sentence expires, unless sooner discharged.

To provide for certain children from Lyman and Industrial schools, etc.

SECTION 6. Whenever in the opinion of the trustees of the Lyman and Industrial schools any children in those schools will be better provided for outside thereof, said trustees shall have the power to release such children on probation, and shall deliver such children into the care and custody of the department for children. Said department shall make all necessary provision for such children, and shall have the same powers and be subject to the same duties with regard to the same as are possessed by or are incumbent upon it in regard to other children in its care and under its control. Upon such delivery to the said department for children, the trustees of the Lyman and Industrial schools shall be relieved from all responsibility in regard to the children so delivered until such children are returned to the said schools by the said department. The said department may, whenever it is deemed best by it, return children so delivered to it to the school from which they came, and when so returned such children shall serve out the term for which they were originally committed to said school unless sooner discharged. All the children who, at the time of the passage of this act, shall be in their usual homes or in any situation or family, having been placed there by the trustees of the Lyman and Industrial schools in accordance with the provisions of sections three and four of chapter four hundred and twenty-eight of the acts of the year eighteen hundred and ninety-five, shall be deemed to have been delivered by the said board of trustees to the said department in accordance with the provisions of this section, and shall be treated by said department in accordance with the above provisions of law.

SECTION 7. Sections three and four of chapter four hundred and twenty-eight of the acts of the year eighteen hundred and ninety-five are hereby repealed. **Repeal. 1895, c. 428, §§ 3, 4.**

SECTION 8. The department shall employ suitable agents to represent it in all the courts and before all the magistrates of the Commonwealth, and it shall be the duty of such agents to investigate into the condition of every child brought before such court or magistrate and to assist the court or magistrate in the disposition of such child. Such agents, when requested by the court or magistrate, shall in regard to juvenile offenders perform all duties prescribed by law for probation officers. They, subject to the direction of the department, may have the custody of such offenders during the whole or any part of the period of probation, and may at any time during such period take such offenders, without warrant, and surrender **To employ agents to represent it in courts, etc.**

them to the court or magistrate permitting the probation. The agents and other officers of the department, moreover, are hereby authorized, whenever requested by any court or magistrate, to serve all criminal process in all cases against alleged juvenile offenders.

Children under twelve years of age to be committed to department, for non-payment of fine.

SECTION 9. Whenever any child under twelve years of age is adjudged guilty of an offence punishable by fine, the court or magistrate, upon non-payment of the fine or costs, or both, shall commit such child to the custody of the department for children for a period not exceeding thirty days, and said department is authorized to make all proper porvisions for the safe keeping of said child.

Children under fourteen years of age, held as witnesses, to be committed to department, etc.

SECTION 10. Whenever any child under fourteen years of age is held as a witness in any case before any court or magistrate, such court or magistrate may commit said child to the custody of the department for children, and said department is authorized to make all proper provisions for the safe keeping of said child, and for his or her presence at the examination or trial for which he or she is held as a witness.

May establish houses for keeping of children, etc.

SECTION 11. The department may establish houses for the keeping of children in its care or custody, and for this purpose it may hire or buy such property as may be necessary. Children who are unfit to be placed in families may be placed in a hospital or in an appropriate institution.

To place children in selected places; powers of transfer, etc.

SECTION 12. The department shall place the children in its care or custody in places or with persons selected or approved by the department, with or without payment of board, and with or without indenture or contract, and, in its discretion, may place such children in their usual homes. The department shall have full power from time to time, whenever it thinks best, to transfer any child in its care or custody to another home, place or person, and said department may discharge from its care, custody or control any child whenever in the opinion of the department such discharge will be for the best interests of such child; and in case of the discharge of any child committed to it, the department shall make an entry upon its records of the name of such child and of the person to whom it is sent, the date of such discharge and the reason therefor, and a copy of such record shall be transmitted to the court, magistrate or other authority by whom such child was committed

SECTION 13. The department shall visit, by itself or by its agents, at least once a year and as much oftener as it shall deem best, all children in its care, custody or control, and it shall keep full records of the surroundings, condition and conduct of each child. To visit children in its care, custody, etc.

SECTION 14. The department shall make such reports and give such information to the state board of charity as the latter board may from time to time require, as to the number and whereabouts of the children in its care, custody and control, and as to its expenditure of money and general work. To make reports to state board of charity.

SECTION 15. Section eighteen of chapter two hundred and fifteen of the Public Statutes is hereby repealed. Repeal. P. S. 215, § 18.

SECTION 16. Section one of chapter three hundred and eighty-two of the acts of the year eighteen hundred and ninety-six is hereby amended in the fourth, fifth, sixth, seventh and eighth lines thereof by striking out the words "state board of lunacy and charity or by the trustees of the Lyman and Industrial schools or kept under the control of either of said boards," and inserting in place thereof the words "department for children or kept under the control of said department." Amendment. 1896, c. 382, § 1.

SECTION 17. The acts and parts of acts specified in the annexed schedule are hereby amended by striking out the words "state board of lunacy and charity," "board of lunacy and charity" and "state board" wherever they occur therein and substituting in place thereof the words "department for children." Amendments.

SCHEDULE OF ACTS AND PARTS OF ACTS AMENDED.

Public Statutes.

Chapter 48, section 27, as amended by statute 1886, chapter 101, section 4. — Of the employment of children and regulations respecting them.

Chapter 84, sections 21, 23. — Of the support of paupers by cities and towns.

Chapter 86, sections 44, 45, 46. — Of alien passengers and state paupers.

Chapter 89, sections 22, 50, 53, 54, 55, 56. — Of the state primary and reform schools and the visitation and reformation of juvenile offenders.

One Thousand Eight Hundred and Eighty-two.

Chapter 127, section 2, as amended by statute 1886, chapter 101, section 4. — An act relating to juvenile offenders.

Chapter 181, sections 2 and 3, as amended by statute 1886, chapter 101, section 4. — An act relating to indigent and neglected children.

Chapter 270, section 3, as amended by statute 1886, chapter 101, section 4, and by statute 1892, chapter 318, section 16. — An act for the better protection of children.

One Thousand Eight Hundred and Eighty-three.

Chapter 110, as amended by statute 1886, chapter 101, section 4. — An act relative to the trial of juvenile offenders.

Chapter 232, section 3, as amended by statute 1886, chapter 101, section 4. — An act relating to indigent and neglected children.

One Thousand Eight Hundred and Eighty-six.

Chapter 330, section 2. — An act relating to indigent and neglected children.

One Thousand Eight Hundred and Eighty-seven.

Chapter 401, section 1, as amended by statute 1893, chapter 197, section 2. — An act relating to the enforcement of the law for placing pauper children in families.

One Thousand Eight Hundred and Eighty-eight.

Chapter 248, section 1. — An act concerning neglected children and juvenile offenders.

One Thousand Eight Hundred and Eighty-nine.

Chapter 309, section 2, as amended by statute 1891, chapter 194. — An act for the better protection of infants.

Chapter 309, section 3. — An act for the better protection of infants.

One Thousand Eight Hundred and Ninety-two.

Chapter 318, sections 1, 3, 4, 5, 6, 7, 8, 9, 12, 13, 14, 15. — An act to provide for the licensing and regulating of boarding houses for infants.

One Thousand Eight Hundred and Ninety-three.

Chapter 217, section 1. — An act relating to indigent and neglected infants in the state almshouse.

Chapter 252, section 1. — An act relating to indigent and neglected children.

One Thousand Eight Hundred and Ninety-five.

Chapter 310, section 1. — An act to provide for the appointment of a special district police officer.

One Thousand Eight Hundred and Ninety-six.

Chapter 382, section 1. — An act relative to the cost of education in the public schools of children under charge of the state board of lunacy and charity or of the trustees of the Lyman and Industrial schools.

The acts and parts of acts specified in the annexed schedule are hereby amended by striking out the word "board" wherever it occurs in the lines named and substituting therefor the word "department."

Schedule of Acts and Parts of Acts amended.

Public Statutes.

Chapter 89, section 22, in the 3d and 7th lines thereof. — Of the state primary and reform schools and the visitation and reformation of juvenile offenders.

One Thousand Eight Hundred and Eighty-two.

Chapter 127, section 2, in the 6th line. — An act relating to juvenile offenders.

Chapter 181, section 3, in the 11th and 17th lines. — An act relating to indigent and neglected children.

Chapter 270, section 3, in the 8th and 9th lines. — An act for the better protection of children.

One Thousand Eight Hundred and Eighty-three.

Chapter 110, in the 11th line. — An act relative to the control of juvenile offenders.

Chapter 232, section 3, in the 8th line. — An act relating to indigent and neglected children.

One Thousand Eight Hundred and Eighty-seven.

Chapter 401, section 1, in the 15th line. — An act relating to the enforcement of the law for placing pauper children in families.

One Thousand Eight Hundred and Eighty-nine.

Chapter 309, section 2, in the 6th line — An act for the better protection of infants.

One Thousand Eight Hundred and Ninety-two.

Chapter 318, section 15, in the 10th line. — An act to provide for the licensing and regulating of boarding houses for infants.

One Thousand Eight Hundred and Ninety-three.

Chapter 217, section 1, in the 5th line. — An act relating to indigent and neglected infants in the state almshouse.

One Thousand Eight Hundred and Ninety-five.

Chapter 310, section 2. — An act to provide for the appointment of a special district police officer.

When to take effect.

SECTION 18. This act shall take effect upon the first day of October, eighteen hundred and ninety-seven, but the members of the department for children may be appointed at any time after the passage of this act, and may appoint agents and officers and assign their duties before the said first day of October, eighteen hundred and ninety-seven.

AN ACT TO PREVENT NEGLECTED CHILDREN FROM BEING SENT TO THE TRUANT SCHOOLS.

Be it enacted, etc., as follows:

State board of charity to transfer certain children from truant schools, etc.

SECTION 1. All children ordered to a truant school under the provisions of section twenty-eight of chapter four hundred and ninety-eight of the acts of the year eighteen hundred and ninety-four shall, upon the passage of this act, be transferred by the state board of charity from the said truant schools to the care and custody of the department for children, and any child so transferred shall be held by the department for children under the original order of commitment of the judge or justice without any further process of law.

St. 1894, c. 498, § 28, amended.

SECTION 2. Section twenty-eight of chapter four hundred and ninety-eight of the acts of the year eighteen hundred and ninety-four is hereby amended in the tenth line thereof by striking out the word "nineteen" and inserting in place thereof the word "twenty-six," and by adding at the end of said section the following words: "or such judge or justice may in his discretion commit such children to the care and custody of the department for children for like terms."

SECTION 3. This act shall take effect upon the first day of July next.

An Act to prevent truants from being sentenced to certain houses of reformation.

Be it enacted, etc., as follows:

Section 1. All persons convicted of being habitual truants or of the offences described in section twelve of chapter forty-eight of the Public Statutes who have been sentenced to houses of reformation established under the provisions of section eighteen of chapter two hundred and twenty of the Public Statutes shall, upon the passage of this act, be transferred by the commissioners of prisons from said houses of reformation to the truant schools. Persons so transferred shall be held in the truant schools under the original order of commitment and without further process of law.

Habitual truants to be transferred from certain houses of reformation, etc.

Section 2. Section nineteen of chapter two hundred and twenty of the Public Statutes is hereby repealed.

P. S. 220, § 19, repealed.

Section 3. This act shall take effect upon its passage.

Appendix B.

An Act to establish the state board of insanity.

Be it enacted, etc., as follows:

Section 1. The governor, with the advice and consent of the council, shall appoint five persons, not more than two of whom shall be physicians, who shall constitute the state board of insanity. The persons so appointed shall hold their offices for five years: *provided*, that the terms of office of the five first appointed shall be so arranged that the term of one shall expire each year. All vacancies in said board, whether occurring by expiration of term or otherwise, shall be filled by the governor, with the advice and consent of the council. Two of the persons so appointed shall be experts in insanity, and shall devote their whole time to the performance of their duties as members of the said board, and shall each receive a salary of five thousand dollars a year and his expenses actually incurred in the performance of his duties. The

State board of insanity, how organized, etc.

other members of the board, including the chairman, who shall be designated by the governor, with the advice and consent of the council, shall receive no salaries, but shall be paid only their necessary expenses actually incurred in the performance of their duties. The members of the board may be removed by the governor, with the advice and consent of the council, for cause.

To appoint its officers, etc.

SECTION 2. The board shall have the power to appoint such agents and subordinate officers as it may deem requisite, and to fix their compensation, subject to the approval of the governor; and the amount paid for the salaries of officers and agents employed by the board shall not exceed the sum appropriated by the legislature for this purpose. The board, unless otherwise provided, may assign any of its powers and duties to agents appointed for the purpose and may execute any of its functions by such agents, or by committees appointed from and by said board. The board shall be provided with rooms at the expense of the state, and shall hold meetings each month, on a day fixed by itself, and at such other times as may be needful. It shall make its own by-laws, and shall make a report of its doings to the governor and council on or before the thirty-first day of December in each year, such report being made up to the thirtieth day of September inclusive.

To make annual report.

SECTION 3. The board shall embody in its report a properly classified and tabulated statement of the receipts and expenses of the said board and of each of the several State institutions under its supervision for the said year, and a corresponding classified and tabulated statement of their estimates for the year ensuing, with its opinion as to the necessity or expediency of appropriations in accordance with said estimates; but this provision shall not apply to estimates for the ordinary expenses of the hospitals or asylums for the insane. Said report shall also present a concise review of the work of the several institutions under the supervision of the board for the year preceding, with such suggestions and recommendations as to the said institutions and as to the general interests of insane persons throughout the Commonwealth as may be deemed expedient.

SECTION 4. The board shall present information embodying the experience of institutions for the insane in this and other countries regarding the best and most successful methods of caring for the insane, and it shall also encourage scientific investigation in the matter and treatment of insanity by the medical staffs of the various institutions under its supervision, and shall publish from time to time bulletins and reports of the scientific and clinical work done therein. To present certain information as to experience, etc.

SECTION 5. The board shall prescribe to the superintendents of the several hospitals and asylums for the insane the forms for statistical returns to be made by them in their annual reports, in relation to the sex, age and nativities of the inmates and the places from which they were sent. It shall also prescribe the form of certificates required of mayors of cities or overseers of the poor of towns when a pauper is sent therefrom to any one of the state hospitals or institutions for the insane, which certificate shall contain such inquiry in relation to the age, parentage, birthplace and former residence of, and other facts relating to, the insane poor person as the board may deem necessary, to which mayors and overseers of the poor shall render true answers, so far as they are able, before the insane poor person is received into any one of the said insane hospitals or institutions. The several cities and towns shall be furnished by the board with blank forms for said certificates. To prescribe certain statistical forms, etc.

SECTION 6. The trustees of the several state hospitals and asylums for the insane shall annually on the thirtieth day of September cause to be made and sent to the board an accurate inventory of the stock and supplies on hand and the amount and value thereof at the hospitals under the following heads: live stock on the farm, produce of the farm on hand, carriages and agricultural implements, machinery and mechanical fixtures, beds and bedding in the inmates' department, other furniture in the inmates' department, personal property of the state in the superintendent's department, ready-made clothing, dry goods, provisions and groceries, drugs and medicine, fuel, library. To receive annual inventory of certain institutions, etc.

SECTION 7. The board shall keep records of all patients and attend to the enforcement of the laws with regard to To keep records of patients and to enforce law of commitments, etc. commitments, and shall keep records of the same, and all institutions under its inspection and supervision shall be obliged to furnish all the information required by the board.

To have supervision of certain institutions, etc. SECTION 8. The board shall have general supervision over all the state hospitals and asylums for the insane and all other institutions and receptacles for the insane or feeble-minded, public or private, the Massachusetts hospital for epileptics, the Massachusetts hospital for dipsomaniacs and inebriates, the Massachusetts school for the feeble-minded, the hospital cottages for children, and of all insane persons who may be placed at board by the trustees of the several hospitals and asylums for the insane; and the said board may, when directed by the governor, assume and exercise the powers of the boards of trustees of said institutions in any matter relating to the management thereof.

To inspect new plans, etc. SECTION 9. The board shall inspect all plans for new buildings, and for the extension, alteration or repair of existing buildings to be used by the Commonwealth as hospitals or asylums for the insane; and no such building, extension or addition shall be hereafter constructed for that purpose unless the plan and specifications for its construction are first approved by the board.

To visit certain institutions, etc. SECTION 10. The board shall visit, by itself or its agents, at least once in every year, all places where the insane poor are supported, and ascertain from actual examination and inquiry whether the laws with respect to such insane poor are properly observed; and shall give such directions as will ensure correctness in the returns required in relation to the insane poor, and may use such means as may be necessary to collect all desired information in regard to their support. Powers of, as to state insane poor, etc. It shall have the same powers relating to the state insane poor who are inmates of the hospitals and asylums for the insane within the Commonwealth and their property as are vested in towns and overseers of the poor in reference to paupers supported or relieved by towns. The board may, moreover, when it has reason to believe that any insane person is deprived of suitable treatment and is confined in an almshouse or other place, make application for the commitment of such person to a state insane hospital, according to the provisions of law.

SECTION 11. The board may transfer insane pauper inmates, including those committed under provisions contained in section fifty of chapter eighty-seven of the Public Statutes, section fifteen of chapter two hundred and thirteen of the Public Statutes, sections sixteen and nineteen of chapter two hundred and fourteen of the Public Statutes and sections ten, twelve and fourteen of chapter two hundred and twenty-two of the Public Statutes, from any one of the state hospitals or asylums for the insane to another state hospital or asylum for the insane, and may transfer and commit inmates of the other state institutions to the state hospitals or asylums for the insane; and it may send any such insane pauper inmates to any state or place where they belong, when the public interest or the necessities of the inmates require such transfer. The names of the inmates so removed shall be entered upon the register of the hospital or asylum for the insane, together with the usual details of their history, and shall be recorded by the several superintendents as discharged by the board for the purpose of removal from the state; but no transfer or commitment shall be made by the board of inmates of other state institutions to the state hospitals and asylums for the insane, except in accordance with the provisions of law regulating the commitment of insane persons.

To make certain transfers of insane persons, etc.

SECTION 12. The board, upon the application of the director, manager or trustees of a private hospital or asylum for the insane, may transfer any inmate of such institution to another private institution, or to a state hospital or asylum for the insane, but no such transfer shall be made without the consent of the legal or natural guardian of such inmate.

To make transfers of insane persons to and from private asylums, when, etc.

SECTION 13. The board shall act as commissioners in insanity, with power to investigate the question of the insanity and condition of any person committed to any hospital or asylum for the insane, public or private, or restrained of his liberty by reason of alleged insanity at any place within this Commonwealth, and shall discharge any person so committed or restrained if, in its opinion, such person is not insane, or can be cared for after such dis-

To act as commissioners in insanity, etc.

charge without danger to others and with benefit to himself or herself.

To visit every hospital and asylum under its supervision at least twice a year.

SECTION 14. The board itself or any two of its members shall visit every hospital and asylum under its supervision at least twice a year, and shall carefully inspect every part of the institution visited, shall offer an opportunity to every patient to hold an interview, shall inspect every certificate of commitment entered or filed since its or their last visitation, and shall enter in a book, provided for that purpose, minutes of the condition of the institution at that time, of the patients therein, of the patients under restraint and their number, and any criticisms or observations that the board or visiting members may have to make, namely, as to the occupation, amusement or classification of the patients, as to the cleanliness and sanitary condition of the institution, as to the diet of the patients, and any other matters that it or they may deem worthy of observation or criticism.

Patients in hospitals, etc., to be allowed to write freely to board, etc.

SECTION 15. All patients in any hospital, asylum or receptacle for the insane shall be allowed, subject to the regulations of the board, to write freely to the board, and letters so written shall be forwarded, unopened, by the superintendent or person in charge of said hospital, asylum or receptacle for the insane, to the said board for such disposition as it shall deem right, and the said board may send any letters or other communications to any patients in any hospital, asylum or receptacle for the insane, whenever it may deem proper so to do.

Nurses to be employed in taking, etc., patients to hospitals, etc.

SECTION 16. The nurses of the insane hospitals or asylums shall be employed, as far as practicable, in taking and transferring patients to and from institutions for the insane, instead of officers of the law.

Superintendent, etc., to notify board of question as to commitment, etc.

SECTION 17. The superintendent or physician in charge of any insane hospital or asylum shall immediately notify the said board if there is any question as to the propriety of the commitment of any person received therein, and said board, upon such notification, shall inquire into the sanity of such patient and into the question of the propriety of the commitment.

To prescribe uniform system of accounts, etc.

SECTION 18. The board shall prescribe a uniform system of keeping accounts in the several state hospitals and asylums under its supervision, and the same shall be adopted and used in those institutions.

SECTION 19. All questions as to the sanity of inmates of the penal, reformatory and other institutions of the Commonwealth who present indications of insanity shall be referred to the board or its officers for determination. To have jurisdiction of questions of sanity of inmates of penal, etc., institutions.

SECTION 20. The board shall prescribe the forms of certificates required by law in the commitments of insane persons to hospitals, asylums and receptacles for the insane and for the commitment of patients to the Massachusetts hospital for dipsomaniacs and inebriates, and such forms when prescribed shall be the sole forms used in such commitments. To prescribe forms of certificates required in commitment of insane persons, etc.

SECTION 21. The board and the several boards of trustees of the different state hospitals and asylums for the insane shall meet quarterly for the purpose of consultation and harmonious action. To meet quarterly with trustees of state hospitals, etc., for insane, etc.

SECTION 22. The board is hereby authorized to discharge patients from the Massachusetts hospital for dipsomaniacs and inebriates, and to transfer the inmates of the said hospital to other state institutions and the inmates of the other state institutions to the said hospital; but no inmate of the other state institutions shall be transferred to said hospital unless he has been duly committed thereto in conformity with the provisions of law governing the commitment of patients to said hospital. To have authority to discharge and transfer patients from Massachusetts hospital for dipsomaniacs, etc.

SECTION 23. The board shall devise, if practicable, a system by which the board of trustees of the Massachusetts hospital for dipsomaniacs and inebriates shall be informed specifically of the history of any person whom it is proposed to commit to said hospital, and by which, if possible, an investigation of the record of such patient shall be made by a probation officer, with a view to informing the court or magistrate prior to his deciding the question of commitment. To devise system to inform trustees of Massachusetts hospital for dipsomaniacs, etc., as to record of patients, etc.

SECTION 24. The word "lunatic," wherever it occurs in the names of the several hospitals and in the laws relating to the insane, is hereby stricken out, and the term "insane" or "insane person" is substituted therefor. Use of word "lunatic" abrogated.

SECTION 25. All the powers possessed by and all the duties incumbent upon the state board of lunacy and Transfer of certain powers to board, etc.

charity, relative to the state hospitals and asylums for the insane and other asylums and receptacles for the insane, public or private, relative to insane persons and as commissioners in lunacy, are hereby taken from the said state board of lunacy and charity and vested in the state board of insanity, and said state board of insanity is hereby authorized and empowered to assume and exercise the same. The said state board of insanity shall succeed to all the rights, powers and duties of the said state board of lunacy and charity in regard to all the insane poor placed in families by the latter board, and the care and custody of the same is hereby transferred to the said state board of insanity without further process of law.

Board to report methods providing for care of insane by state, etc.

SECTION 26. The board shall report to the legislature on or before the first day of March in the year eighteen hundred and ninety-eight such method or methods as in its opinion shall be the best to provide for the care of the insane poor who, according to the provisions of this act, will be placed on the first day of October in the year eighteen hundred and ninety-eight in the care and custody of the Commonwealth. In such report the board shall include a statement of what building or buildings are needed to accommodate such insane persons and any other suggestions that may occur to it in relation thereto as advisable to present for the consideration of the legislature.

Care, etc., of insane poor vested in the state.

SECTION 27. The care, custody and control of all insane persons who are supported at public expense is hereby vested in the Commonwealth, whether they have a settlement therein or not, and the Commonwealth shall relieve and support all such persons and defray the expenses thereof.

Insane poor to be committed to hospital, etc., maintained by state or boarded out.

SECTION 28. All insane persons dependent upon public charity within the Commonwealth, whether they have a settlement therein or not, shall be committed to some hospital, asylum or receptacle for the insane maintained by the Commonwealth; but nothing herein contained shall prevent the state board of insanity from placing insane persons at board in accordance with the provisions of chapter three hundred and eighty-five of the acts of the year eighteen hundred and eighty-five.

SECTION 29. The state board of insanity may transfer all insane persons dependent upon public charity who may, upon this act taking effect, be in institutions for the insane maintained by the several cities and towns of the Commonwealth, and who have settlements within those cities and towns, to the state hospitals, asylums and receptacles for the insane.

Board may transfer insane persons from city institutions for the insane.

SECTION 30. The state board of insanity is hereby authorized to take by purchase or otherwise, in the name and behalf of the Commonwealth, the whole or any part of the lands and buildings owned by the several cities of the Commonwealth and established and maintained therein as asylums for the care and treatment of the insane, or may lease the same for such term and for such rent as the state board of insanity shall deem best. In the event of the taking of said lands and buildings by said board in the name and behalf of the Commonwealth, the said state board shall file in the registry of deeds for the county and district within which the said lands and buildings are situated a description of the lands and buildings so taken, with a statement, signed by said board or a majority thereof, that the same are taken under the provisions of this act, in the name and behalf of the Commonwealth, and the act and time of filing thereof shall be deemed to be the act and time of the taking of such lands and buildings, and be a sufficient notice to all persons that the same have been so taken. The title to all the lands and buildings so taken shall vest absolutely in the Commonwealth and its assigns forever. The Commonwealth shall be liable to pay all damages which shall be sustained by any city by reason of the taking of such lands and buildings. Said state board shall have full power, subject to the approval of the governor and council, to settle by agreement or arbitration the value of the lands and buildings taken as aforesaid, and if not so settled, the value may be assessed by a jury at the bar of the superior court for the county in which the lands and buildings are situated, upon petition to be filed in the office of the clerk of said court by the city owning said lands and buildings within one year after such taking and not afterwards.

Board may take lands, etc., owned by cities for asylums for the insane.

Amendment. St. 1886, 298, § 9.

SECTION 31. Section nine of chapter two hundred and ninety-eight of the acts of the year eighteen hundred and eighty-six is hereby amended by striking out in the third line the words "board of education" and inserting in place thereof the words "state board of insanity."

Amendment. St. 1885, 385, § 3.

SECTION 32. Section three of chapter three hundred and eighty-five of the acts of the year eighteen hundred and eighty-five, as amended by section four of chapter one hundred and one of the acts of the year eighteen hundred and eighty-six, is hereby amended by striking out the words "board of lunacy and charity" wherever they occur therein, and substituting therefor the words "state board of insanity."

Amendments.

SECTION 33. The acts and parts of acts specified in the annexed schedule are hereby amended by striking out the words "lunacy and charity" wherever they occur therein, and substituting in place thereof the word "insanity."

SCHEDULE OF ACTS AND PARTS OF ACTS AMENDED.

Public Statutes.

Chapter 87, section 1, as amended by statute 1886, chapter 101, section 4, in the 1st line thereof. — Of lunacy and institutions for the insane.

Chapter 87, section 12, as amended by statute 1894, chapter 195, in the 12th and 13th lines thereof. — Of lunacy and institutions for lunatics.

One Thousand Eight Hundred and Eighty-four.

Chapter 322, sections 7 and 9, as amended by statute 1886, chapter 101, section 4. — An act to establish a homeopathic hospital for the insane.

One Thousand Eight Hundred and Eighty-five.

Chapter 385, section 1, as amended by statute 1886, chapter 101, section 4. — An act providing for the care of certain insane persons.

One Thousand Eight Hundred and Eighty-six.

Chapter 298, sections 1 and 2. — An act concerning the Massachusetts school for the feeble-minded.

Chapter 319, sections 1, 2, 3, as amended by statute 1890, chapter 414, section 2. — An act concerning the commitment and custody of insane persons.

One Thousand Eight Hundred and Eighty-seven.

Chapter 346, section 2, as amended by statute 1896, chapter 482. — An act concerning commitments and transfers of the insane.

One Thousand Eight Hundred and Eighty-nine.

Chapter 414, section 16, as amended by statute 1891, chapter 158. — An act to establish the Massachusetts hospital for dipsomaniacs and inebriates.

One Thousand Eight Hundred and Ninety-two.

Chapter 425, section 4. — An act to provide for the building of an asylum for the chronic insane.

One Thousand Eight Hundred and Ninety-five.

Chapter 286, section 2. — An act relative to the commitment of insane persons.

Chapter 390, sections 5 and 6. — An act to establish an asylum for insane criminals at Bridgewater and to regulate commitments and removals to the same.

Chapter 483, sections 10 and 11. — An act to establish the Massachusetts hospital for epileptics.

SECTION 34. Chapter two hundred and thirty-four of the acts of the year eighteen hundred and eighty-four is hereby repealed. **Repeal of St. 1884, 234.**

SECTION 35. All the provisions of this act, except those hereinafter enumerated, shall take effect upon the first day of July, eighteen hundred and ninety-seven; but the members of the said state board may be appointed at any time after the passage of this act, and may appoint agents and officers and assign their duties before the said first day of July. The provisions of sections twenty-seven and twenty-eight shall take effect on the first day of October, eighteen hundred and ninety-eight. **When to take effect.**

APPENDIX C.

AN ACT CONCERNING THE SETTLEMENT OF PAUPERS.

Be it enacted, etc., as follows:

SECTION 1. Legal settlements may be acquired in any city or town, so as to oblige such place to relieve and support the persons acquiring the same, in case they are **Legal settlements, how acquired.**

poor and stand in need of relief, in the manner following and not otherwise, namely: —

First. Any person, male or female, of the age of twenty-one years, who resides in any place within this state for three years together, shall thereby gain a settlement in such place.

Second. The provisions of the preceding clause shall apply to married women who have not a settlement derived by marriage under the provisions of the third clause, and to widows.

Third. A married woman shall follow and have the settlement of her husband, if he has any within the state; otherwise her own at the time of marriage, if she then had any, shall not be lost or suspended by the marriage.

Fourth. Legitimate children, until they gain a settlement of their own, shall follow and have the settlement of their parents or surviving parent, or of the parent to whom such children are awarded in case of divorce, if the parent or parents have any settlement within the state.

Fifth. Illegitimate children shall follow and have the settlement of their mother at the time of their birth if she then has any within the state; but neither legitimate nor illegitimate children shall gain a settlement by birth in the place where they are born, if neither of their parents then has a settlement therein.

Sixth. Any person who was duly enlisted and mustered into the military or naval service of the United States, as a part of the quota of any city or town in this Commonwealth, under any call of the president of the United States during the late civil war, or duly assigned as a part of the quota thereof after having been enlisted and mustered into said service, and who duly served for not less than one year, or died or became disabled from wounds or disease received or contracted while engaged in such service, or while a prisoner in the hands of the enemy, and his wife or widow and minor children, shall be deemed thereby to have acquired a settlement in such place; and any person who would otherwise be entitled to a settlement under this clause, but who was not a part of the quota of any city or town, shall, if he served as a part of the quota of the Commonwealth, be deemed to have acquired a settlement in the place where he actually resided at the time of his enlistment. But these provisions shall not apply to any person who was enlisted and received a bounty for such enlistment in more than one place, unless the second enlistment was made after an honorable discharge from the first term of service, nor to any person who has been proved guilty of wilful desertion, or who left the service otherwise than by reason of disability or an honorable discharge.

Seventh. Upon the division of a city or town, every person having a legal settlement therein, but being absent at the time of such division and not having acquired a legal settlement elsewhere, shall have his legal settlement in that place wherein his last dwelling-place or home happens to fall upon such division; and when a new city or town is incorporated, composed of a part of one or more incorporated places, every person legally settled in the places of which such new city or town is so composed, and who actually dwells and has his home within the bounds of such new city or town at the time of its incorporation, and any person duly qualified as provided in the sixth clause of this section, who, at the time of his enlistment, dwelt and had his home within such bounds, shall thereby acquire a legal settlement in such new place; but no person residing in that part of a place which upon such division is incorporated into a new city or town, and having then no legal settlement therein, shall acquire any by force of such incorporation only; nor shall such incorporation prevent his acquiring a settlement therein within the time and by the means by which he would have gained it there if no such division had been made.

Settlement not acquired while receiving relief as pauper.

SECTION 2. Nothing in the preceding section shall be construed to give to any person the right to acquire a settlement or to be in process of acquiring a settlement while receiving relief as a pauper, unless within three years from the time of receiving such relief he reimburses the cost thereof to the city or town furnishing the same.

Inability to maintain wife, etc., in hospital, etc., for insane not to make one a pauper.

SECTION 3. No person who actually supports himself and his family shall be deemed to be a pauper by reason of the commitment of his wife, child or other relative to a hospital or asylum for the insane or other institution of charity, reform or correction, by order of a court or magistrate, and of his inability to maintain such wife, child or relative therein; but nothing herein contained shall be construed to release him from liability for such maintenance.

Provision for persons who have begun to acquire settlements.

SECTION 4. No person who has begun to acquire a settlement by the laws in force at and before the time when this chapter takes effect, in any of the ways in which any time is prescribed for a residence, or for the continuance or succession of any other act, shall be prevented or delayed by the provisions hereof; but he shall acquire a settlement by a continuance or succession of the same residence or other act, in the same time and manner as if the former laws had continued in force.

Settlements to continue, etc.

SECTION 5. Except as hereinafter provided, every legal settlement shall continue till it is lost or defeated by acquiring a new one within this state, and upon acquiring such new settlement all former settlements shall be defeated and lost.

Acquired under laws in force prior to May 13, 1865.

SECTION 6. All settlements acquired by virtue of any provision of law in force prior to the thirteenth day of May in the year eighteen hundred and sixty-five are hereby defeated and lost, except where the existence of such settlement prevented a subsequent acquisition of settlement in the same place under the provisions of this act or under corresponding provisions in other statutes existing prior to the passage hereof; and *provided*, that whenever a settlement acquired by marriage has been thus defeated the former settlement of the wife, if not defeated by the same provision, shall be thereby revived.

Lost by absence from state for ten years, etc.

SECTION 7. All persons absent from the state for ten years consecutively shall thereby lose their settlements.

Repeal of P. S. 83.

SECTION 8. Chapter eighty-three of the Public Statutes is hereby repealed, saving all acts done, or rights accruing, accrued or established, or proceedings, doings or acts ratified or confirmed, or suits or proceedings had or commenced before the repeal takes effect.

When to take effect.

SECTION 9. This act shall take effect upon the first day of January in the year eighteen hundred and ninety-eight.

Appendix D.

An Act in relation to the Massachusetts hospital for dipsomaniacs and inebriates.

Be it enacted, etc., as follows:

Section 1. The board of trustees of the Massachusetts hospital for dipsomaniacs and inebriates are hereby authorized, whenever in their judgment a patient has been long enough in the hospital to enable them to form an opinion as to whether or not the treatment would benefit him, to finally discharge such patient. **Trustees of Massachusetts hospital for dipsomaniacs, etc., may finally discharge patients.**

Section 2. This act shall take effect upon its passage.

Appendix E.

An Act to create the state board of charity.

Be it enacted, etc., as follows:

Section 1. The governor, with the advice and consent of the council, shall appoint seven persons, who shall constitute the state board of charity. **State board of charity, how organized, etc.** The persons so appointed shall hold their office for seven years, provided the terms of office of the seven first appointed shall be so arranged that the term of one shall expire each year. All vacancies in said board, whether occurring by expiration of term or otherwise, shall be filled by the governor, with the advice and consent of the council. One of the persons so appointed shall be designated by the governor with the advice and consent of the council as the secretary of the board, who shall devote his entire time to the performance of the duties of his office, and shall receive a salary of thirty-five hundred dollars a year and his expenses actually incurred in the performance of his duties. The other members of the board, including the chairman, who shall be designated by the governor with the advice and consent of the council, shall receive no salaries, but shall be paid only their necessary expenses actually incurred in the performance of their duties. The members of the board may be removed by the governor with the advice and consent of the council for cause.

To appoint agents, etc.; make by-laws, etc.

SECTION 2. The board shall have the power to appoint such agents and subordinate officers as it may deem requisite, and to fix their compensation, subject to the approval of the governor, and the amount paid for the salaries of officers and agents employed by the board shall not exceed the sum appropriated by the legislature for this purpose; and the board may assign any of its powers and duties to agents appointed for the purpose, and may execute any of its functions by such agents or by committees appointed from and by said board. The board shall be provided with rooms at the expense of the state, and shall hold meetings each month on a day fixed by itself and at such other times as may be needful. It shall make its own by-laws, and shall make a report of its doings to the governor and council on or before the thirty-first day of December in each year, such report being made up to the thirtieth day of September inclusive.

Annual report.

SECTION 3. The board shall embody in its report a properly classified and tabulated statement of the receipts and expenses of the said board and of each of the several state institutions under its supervision for the said year, and a corresponding classified and tabulated statement of their estimates for the year ensuing, with its opinion as to the necessity or expediency of appropriations in accordance with said estimates. Said report shall also present a concise review of the work of the several institutions under its supervision for the year preceding, with such suggestions and recommendations as to said institutions and as to the general charitable interests of the Commonwealth as may be deemed expedient.

To prepare tables, and to prescribe certain forms.

SECTION 4. The board shall prepare, from the returns made by the overseers of the poor of the several towns, tables of all the sane poor supported by towns, and shall print in its annual report the most important information thus obtained. The board shall prescribe to the superintendents of the several institutions under its supervision the form for statistical returns to be made by them in their annual reports in relation to the sex, age and nativities of the inmates and the places from which they were sent.

It shall also prescribe the form of certificate required of mayors of cities or overseers of the poor of towns when a pauper is sent therefrom to any one of the state institutions under its supervision, which certificate shall contain such inquiry in relation to the age, parentage, birthplace, former residence of, and other facts relating to the sane pauper person as the board may deem necessary, to which mayors and overseers of the poor shall render true answers, so far as they are able, before the sane poor person is received into any one of the said institutions. The several cities and towns shall be furnished by the board with blank forms for said certificates.

SECTION 5. The board shall have the general supervision of the sane poor at the state almshouse and at the state farm until such time as the latter shall be placed under the supervision of the commissioners of prisons, of the Lyman school for boys and of the Industrial school for girls. It shall also have the general supervision of the department for children, the county and municipal reformatories and homes for children, city and town almshouses, tramp houses and receptacles for tramps or vagrants, and it shall visit the state institutions above named at least as often as once a month. **To have general supervision of certain institutions, etc.**

SECTION 6. The board shall visit at least once in every year all places where the state sane poor are supported, and ascertain from actual examination and inquiry whether the laws in regard to such poor persons are properly observed, and shall give such directions as will ensure correctness in the returns required in relation to paupers; and it shall have the same powers relating to the state sane poor who are inmates of the state almshouse and to their property as are vested in towns and overseers of the poor in reference to paupers supported or relieved by towns. **To visit places where state sane poor are supported, etc.**

SECTION 7. The board shall have charge of the interests of the state upon the subject of charity generally, and shall investigate the causes of pauperism and existing and proposed methods and practices in the administration of relief of the poor. It shall publish from time to time information on the work of public and private charitable agencies in other states and countries, so far as the same **To have charge of interests of state upon subject of charity, etc.**

may be applicable to the needs of this Commonwealth, and it shall publish, periodically or otherwise, bulletins to be distributed to public officials and to other persons, and shall establish a bureau of information for persons engaged or interested in public or private charities, and shall also promote all measures designed to procure a uniform policy in the treatment of tramps and vagrants throughout the Commonwealth.

To determine questions of settlement of the poor, etc.

Section 8. The board shall determine all questions relating to the settlement or non-settlement of the state poor coming under the control of the state institutions under its supervision and under the supervision of the state board of insanity, and shall administer the laws of settlement relating to the support of the state sane poor by cities and towns, and shall prosecute all cases of bastardy of non-settled persons.

May transfer inmates of certain institutions, etc.

Section 9. The board may transfer sane pauper inmates from one state institution under its supervision to another, and may send such paupers to any state or place where they belong, when the public interest or the necessities of the inmates require such transfer.

Trustees of certain institutions to send account of stock, etc., to state board, etc.

Section 10. The trustees of the several institutions under the supervision of the board shall annually on the thirtieth day of September cause to be made and sent to the board an accurate account of the stock and supplies on hand and the amount and value thereof at the institutions, under the following heads: live stock on the farm, produce of the farm on hand, carriages and agricultural implements, machinery and mechanical fixtures, beds and bedding in the inmates' department, other furniture in the inmates' department, personal property of the state in the superintendent's department, ready-made clothing, dry goods, provisions and groceries, drugs and medicine, fuel, library.

To advise and suggest as to plans and estimates for new buildings, etc.

Section 11. All plans or estimates for new sites and new buildings, for the extension, alteration or repair of existing buildings, for the arrangement of grounds or systems of sewerage, or for heating with reference to buildings which are, or will be when completed, subject to the visitation of the board, shall before adoption be submitted to the board for its advice and suggestion.

SECTION 12. The state board of lunacy and charity is hereby abolished, and all the powers possessed by and all the duties incumbent upon the board so abolished relative to the state almshouse, state farm, the Lyman school for boys and the industrial school for girls, and other charitable interests and institutions, except where otherwise expressly provided, and relative to the sane poor within the Commonwealth, are hereby vested in the said board of charity, and all the laws applying to the above duties and powers of the said state board of lunacy and charity shall apply to the said state board of charity. State board of lunacy and charity abolished, etc.

SECTION 13. Section eighteen of chapter eighty-four as amended by section one of chapter ninety of the acts of the year eighteen hundred and ninety-one, in the twelfth line thereof; section two of chapter eighty-five, in the fourth line thereof; section one of chapter eighty-six, in the third line thereof; section four of chapter eighty-eight, in the first line thereof; section sixty-eight of chapter two hundred and twenty, in the eighth line thereof, of the Public Statutes, all as amended by section four of chapter one hundred and one of the acts of the year eighteen hundred and eighty-six; section four of chapter two hundred and ninety-seven of the acts of the year eighteen hundred and eighty-four, the latter as amended by section four of chapter one hundred and one of the acts of the year eighteen hundred and eighty-six, in the third line thereof; section two of chapter two hundred and ninety-two of the acts of the year eighteen hundred and eighty-seven, in the first line thereof; section two of chapter two hundred and seventy-eight of the acts of the year eighteen hundred and ninety, in the fifth line thereof, — are hereby amended by striking out the words "lunacy and," wherever they occur in said lines. Amendments.

SECTION 14. Section nine of chapter seventy-nine of the Public Statutes, as amended by chapter three hundred and sixty-seven of the acts of the year eighteen hundred and eighty-seven, is hereby repealed. Repeal. P. S. 79, § 9.

SECTION 15. This act shall take effect on the first day of July in the year eighteen hundred and ninety-seven; but the members of said state board of charity may be When to take effect.

appointed at any time after the passage of this act, and may appoint agents and officers and assign their duties before the said first day of July.

Appendix F.

An Act giving the state control of all prisons.

Be it enacted, etc., as follows:

State to maintain jails and houses of correction, etc.

Section 1. The jails and houses of correction now maintained by the several counties shall be hereafter maintained by the Commonwealth. The cost of such maintenance shall be paid from the treasury of the Commonwealth, and all money received by any jailer, superintendent or master of a house of correction, which under existing laws would be payable to the treasurer of the county, shall be paid into the treasury of the Commonwealth.

State board may take certain lands, etc.

Section 2. The state board of prison commissioners is hereby authorized to take by purchase or otherwise, in the name and behalf of the Commonwealth, the whole or any part of the lands and buildings owned by the several counties and used for and in connection with the jails and houses of correction thereof. Said board shall file in the registry of deeds for the county and district within which the property to be taken is situated, and cause to be recorded therein, a description of any lands and buildings so taken as certain as is required in an ordinary conveyance of land, with a statement, signed by said board or a majority thereof, that the same are taken under the provisions of this act, in the name and behalf of the Commonwealth, and the act and time of filing thereof shall be the act and time of the taking of such lands and buildings and be sufficient notice to all persons that the same have been so taken. The title to all lands and buildings so taken shall vest absolutely in the Commonwealth and its assigns forever. The Commonwealth shall be liable to pay all damages which shall be sustained by any county by reason of the taking of such lands and buildings. Said board shall have full power, subject to the approval of the governor and council, to settle by agreement or arbitration the value of the lands and buildings so taken, and if not so settled, the value may be assessed by a jury at the bar of the superior court for the county in which the lands and buildings taken are situated, upon petition to be filed by the county commissioners for that county in the office of the clerk of said court within one year of said taking and not afterwards.

SECTION 3. The officers of each of said jails and houses of correction so belonging to the Commonwealth, when separate, shall be one superintendent, one deputy superintendent, one chaplain and one physician, and such other officers as may be approved by the state board of prison commissioners. When the jail and house of correction are in one and the same building there may be one set of officers for both of said institutions. **Officers of jails and houses of correction.**

SECTION 4. The superintendent, the physician and the chaplain for each of said prisons shall be appointed by the governor, with the advice and consent of the council, upon the nomination of the state board, and shall hold office during the pleasure of the governor and council. **Officers, how appointed.**

SECTION 5. All other officers of the said prisons shall be appointed by the superintendent, subject to the approval of the state board, and shall hold their offices during the pleasure of the superintendent and the state board. In case of a disagreement between the superintendent and the commissioners in relation to the removal of such officer, the subject may be referred to the governor and council, who may make such removal. **Subordinate officers, how appointed.**

SECTION 6. The salaries of the superintendent, deputy superintendent, chaplain and physician shall be fixed in each case by the state board, subject to the approval of the governor and council. All other officers shall receive such salary as the superintendent of each prison shall determine, subject to the approval of the state board. **Salaries of officers.**

SECTION 7. The superintendent of each of the said prisons shall receive and securely keep, according to the terms of his sentence, any person committed thereto upon a sentence imposed by any court of the United States, or any prisoner sentenced by any such court who may be removed thereto from any other prison. **Superintendents to receive United States prisoners, etc.**

SECTION 8. The superintendent of each of said prisons shall have the custody, rule and charge of all the **Superintendents to have custody, etc., of prisoners.**

prisoners committed to said prison, and shall have the management and direction of the said prison under the rules and regulations made in regard thereto by the state board of prison commissioners. He shall, before entering upon the duties of his office, give to the treasurer of the Commonwealth a bond in such sum and with such sureties as the governor and council shall approve, conditioned that he shall faithfully account for all the money placed in his hands and for the faithful performance of his duties. He shall purchase all supplies necessary for the said prison, shall receive and pay out all moneys paid from the treasury of the Commonwealth for the support thereof, and shall have the custody and control of the buildings and property of the Commonwealth connected therewith. He shall cause to be kept in suitable books a full and accurate statement of the property, expenses, income and business of the said prison under his charge, and he shall make to the state board such reports as it shall require of him.

Powers, etc., of deputy when office of superintendent is vacant, etc.

SECTION 9. When the office of superintendent is vacant in any of said prisons, or the superintendent is absent from the prison under his control or unable to perform the duties of his office, the deputy superintendent shall have the powers, perform the duties and be subject to the obligations and liabilities of the superintendent.

Deputy superintendents to give bonds, when, etc.

SECTION 10. If the office of superintendent in any of said prisons becomes vacant, the state board may require the deputy superintendent to assume the duties of superintendent, and to give a bond to the Commonwealth in a sum to be fixed by the state board, with sufficient sureties, to be approved by it, conditioned for the faithful performance of the duties incumbent upon him as deputy superintendent until the superintendent is appointed, and that he will faithfully account for all moneys which shall come into his hands. In such case and from the time said bond is approved, the deputy superintendent shall, so long as he performs the duties of superintendent, receive the salary of that officer in lieu of his salary as deputy superintendent. If the deputy superintendent does not give such bond when required, the state board may relieve him from the duties of superintendent and appoint a superintendent pro tempore, who shall give such bond and shall have the power and authority to perform the duties and receive the salary of the superintendent until the superintendent is duly appointed and enters upon the discharge of the duties of the office.

SECTION 11. The salaries and pay of all officers and employees in each of said prisons and all bills for supplies and other expenditures for said prisons shall be paid monthly from the treasury of the Commonwealth, the same having first been certified by the auditor of the Commonwealth upon schedules accompanied by vouchers enumerating the bills and pay rolls. Said schedules shall be certified by the superintendent of each prison and approved in each case by the state board. A full record of the pay rolls and bills shall be kept by the superintendent of each prison, and the originals shall be deposited with the auditor of the Commonwealth as vouchers.

Salaries of officers, how paid, etc.

SECTION 12. The superintendent of each prison shall annually make to the state board, on or before the first day of November, a report of the affairs of the prison under his control, including a detailed statement of the receipts and expenses of the year ending on the thirtieth day of September, with such other facts and such recommendations as he shall desire to present, and such report, together with the recommendations of the said state board, shall be included by it in its annual report.

Superintendent of each prison to make annual report, etc.

SECTION 13. All the powers possessed by and all the duties incumbent upon the sheriffs of the several counties and the several jailers, masters of houses of correction and superintendents of houses of industry and workhouses, and the institutions commissioner of the city of Boston, in relation to the custody, rule and charge of the jails, houses of correction, houses of industry and workhouses and of all prisoners therein, are hereby taken from said officers and vested in the superintendents of the jails and houses of correction hereinbefore provided for, and the said superintendents are hereby authorized and empowered to assume and exercise the same, and all persons now in said jails, houses of correction, houses of industry or workhouses are hereby transferred to the custody, rule and charge of the said superintendents. This transfer shall not in any way impair the commitment of any

Powers, etc., of sheriffs, etc., as to jails, etc., transferred to superintendents, etc.

person committed to said jails, houses of correction, houses of industry and workhouses, but said persons shall be held by said superintendents in the prisons severally in their charge under the original warrant, mittimus or other process without further process of law.

Persons committed to jail or house of correction to be delivered to superintendent, etc.

SECTION 14. All persons committed to a jail or house of correction by any process of law shall be delivered to the superintendent or other officer in charge of such jail or house of correction, and said superintendent shall thereupon assume the custody, rule and charge of such persons and shall be solely responsible therefor.

When to take effect.

SECTION 15. This act, except section two thereof, shall take effect on the first day of October of the year eighteen hundred and ninety-eight. Section two shall take effect on the first day of July next.

AN ACT TO CREATE A STATE BOARD OF PRISON COMMISSIONERS.

Be it enacted, etc., as follows:

State board of prison commissioners, how organized, etc.

SECTION 1. The governor, with the advice and consent of the council, shall appoint five persons, who shall constitute the state board of prison commissioners. The persons so appointed shall hold their office for five years, provided the terms of office of the five first appointed shall be so arranged that the term of one shall expire each year. All vacancies in said board, whether occurring by expiration of term or otherwise, shall be filled by the governor, with the advice and consent of the council. Two of the persons so appointed shall receive a salary of five thousand dollars a year each and their expenses actually incurred in the performance of their duties, and shall devote the whole of their time to the performance of their duties as members of said board. The other members of the board shall receive no salaries, but shall be paid only their necessary expenses actually incurred in the performance of their duties. The members of the board may be removed by the governor, with the advice and consent of the council, for cause.

SECTION 2. The board of commissioners of prisons is hereby abolished. Board of commissioners of prisons abolished.

SECTION 3. The state board of prison commissioners shall have all the powers and duties and may exercise all the functions of the board abolished by section two of this act; and said board may assign any of its powers and duties to agents appointed for the purpose, and may execute any of its functions by such agents or by committees appointed from or by said board; and all laws applying to the board hereby abolished shall apply to the board created by section one of this act. Powers and duties of state board of prison commissioners.

SECTION 4. The board shall exercise all the powers and be subject to all the duties now incumbent upon the county commissioners of the several counties and the institutions commissioner of the city of Boston relating to the release of prisoners on permits to be at liberty. The said board shall, moreover, have all the powers and be subject to all the duties and may exercise all the functions heretofore possessed by and incumbent upon the county commissioners of the several counties and the said institutions commissioner in regard to jails and houses of correction which have not been elsewhere expressly given by law to the superintendents of the several jails and houses of correction. Id.

SECTION 5. The board shall have the general supervision of all the jails and houses of correction of the Commonwealth, and shall have the same powers and be subject to the same duties with regard to such prisons in all respects as they will have and be subject to in regard to the other prisons of the Commonwealth when this act shall take effect. Board to have supervision of jails, etc.

SECTION 6. The board shall present to the legislature during the month of February next a report upon the best method of classifying and using the prisons of the several counties regardless of county lines, and of classifying the inmates of said prisons, with a view to securing as far as possible a separation of the different classes of prisoners and the most efficient administration of the prisons, the separation of the sexes, having regard to economy of management and the well-being of the prisoners. They Board to present to legislature during February next report upon classifying prisoners, etc.

shall also present a draft of a bill which will provide for carrying out the suggestions of said report.

Amendment. P. S. 220, § 66.

Section 7. Section sixty-six of chapter two hundred and twenty of the Public Statutes is hereby amended in the first and second lines thereof by striking out the words "county commissioners or directors of a house of correction, house of industry or workhouse," and inserting in place thereof the words "state board of prison commissioners," and in the third line thereof by striking out the word "there" and inserting after the word "confined" the words "in a house of correction, house of industry or workhouse," in the sixth line thereof by striking out the word "they" and inserting in place thereof "said board," and in the twelfth line therereof by striking out the words "commissioners or directors" and inserting in place thereof the words "the said state board," so that said section shall read as follows: "*Section 66.* When it appears to the state board of prison commissioners that a person confined in a house of correction, house of industry or workhouse on conviction before a trial justice, or police, district, or municipal court, of either of the offences mentioned in section twenty-nine of chapter two hundred and seven, has reformed and is willing and desirous to return to an orderly course of life, said state board may by a written order discharge him from confinement, upon condition that if he shall at any time thereafter be convicted of any crime he shall serve the remainder of his original sentence in addition to the sentence then imposed. A person committed by the superior court for either of said offences may be discharged by said court upon recommendation of the said state board upon the same condition."

Amendment. P. S. 220, § 67.

Section 8. Section sixty-seven of chapter two hundred and twenty of the Public Statutes, as amended by chapter two hundred and forty-five of the acts of the year eighteen hundred and eighty-nine, and by section sixteen of chapter four hundred and forty-nine of the acts of the year eighteen hundred and ninety-five, is hereby amended in the first and second lines thereof by striking out the words "county commissioners or in the city of Boston the institutions commissioner," and inserting in place thereof the words "state board of prison commissioners," in the third line by striking out the word "the" before "house" and inserting in place thereof the word "a," in the fourth line thereof by striking out the words "and the directors," in the fifth line by striking out the words "may discharge any person committed to such institution," in the ninth and tenth lines thereof by striking out the words "commissioners and directors" and inserting in place thereof the words "state board," and in the nineteenth line by striking out the words "commissioners or directors" and inserting in place thereof the words "state board," so that the same shall read as follows: "*Section 67.* After six months from the time of sentence the state board of prison commissioners may discharge any person committed to a house of correction, workhouse or house of industry under section thirty-seven of chapter two hundred and seven, upon being satisfied that the convict has reformed, or may bind out such person for any term during the period of sentence as an apprentice or servant to any inhabitant of this state; and said state board and the master, mistress, apprentice and servant shall respectively have all the rights and privileges and be subject to all the duties set forth in chapter one hundred and forty-nine in the same manner as if such binding were made by the overseers of the poor; and the relations between the parties shall not be affected by the age of the party bound. If the master or mistress is discharged from the contract of service or apprenticeship as provided in said chapter, the person bound shall be returned to the place of confinement and serve out the original sentence if any portion thereof is unexpired, but the state board shall not be liable to the costs of the process provided in said chapter."

SECTION 9. Section sixty-eight of chapter two hundred and twenty of the Public Statutes, as amended by chapter two hundred and forty-five of the acts of the year eighteen hundred and eighty-nine, and by section sixteen of chapter four hundred and forty-nine of the acts of the year eighteen hundred and ninety-five, is hereby amended by striking out the words "county commissioners or in

Amendment. P. S. 220, § 68.

the county of Suffolk the institutions commissioner," and inserting in place thereof the words "state board of prison commissioners," in the fourth line thereof by striking out the words "in their respective jurisdictions," in the fifth line thereof by striking out the word "they" and inserting in place thereof the words "the said state board," in the sixth line thereof by striking out the words "the board that has issued such permit" and inserting in place thereof the words "said state board," and in the ninth line thereof by striking out the words "commissioners of prisons" and inserting in place thereof the words "state board of prison commissioners," so that said section shall read as follows: "*Section 68.* When it appears to the state board of prison commissioners that a person imprisoned for drunkenness in a jail, house of correction or other place of confinement has reformed, said state board may issue to him a permit to be at liberty during the remainder of his term of sentence and said state board may revoke the same at any time previous to the expiration of the original term of sentence. The state board of charity and the state board of prison commissioners may issue to persons confined for like offences in the state farm and the reformatory prison for women respectively the permits authorized by this section, and may revoke the same.

Amendment. P. S. 220, § 69.

SECTION 10. Section sixty-nine of chapter two hundred and twenty of the Public Statutes, as amended by chapter two hundred and forty-five of the acts of the year eighteen hundred and eighty-nine, and section sixteen of chapter four hundred and forty-nine of the acts of the year eighteen hundred and ninety-five, is hereby amended in the first, second and third lines thereof by striking out the words "county commissioners of the county in which he is appointed or in Suffolk county of the institutions commissioner" and inserting in place thereof the words "state board or prison commissioners," in the thirteenth line thereof by striking out the words "county commissioners or the said board of directors" and inserting in place thereof the words "said state board," and by striking out in the same line the word "they" and inserting in place thereof the word "it," in the fifteenth line thereof by striking out the word "they" and inserting in place thereof the word "it," in the seventeenth and eighteenth lines thereof by striking out the words "county commissioners or the said board of directors" and inserting in place thereof the words "said state board," and in the nineteenth line thereof by striking out the word "them" and inserting in place thereof the word "it," so that the said section shall read as follows: "*Section 69.* A probation officer may, with the consent of the state board of prison commissioners, investigate the case of any person imprisoned in a jail or house of correction for an offence other than a felony upon sentence of not more than six months or upon a longer sentence of which not more than six months remain unexpired, with a view to ascertaining the probability of the reformation of such person if released from imprisonment. If after such investigation the probation officer recommends the release of the prisoner, and the court which imposed the sentence, or in case of the superior court, the district attorney, certifies a concurrence in such recommendation, the said state board may, if it deem it expedient, release him upon probation, upon such conditions as it deems best and may require a bond for the fulfilment of such conditions. The surety upon such bond may at any time take and surrender his principal, and the said state board may at any time order any prisoner released by it upon probation to return to the prison from which he was released. This section shall not apply to persons held upon sentences of the courts of the United States.

SECTION 11. Section seventy-one of chapter two hundred and twenty of the Public Statutes is hereby amended in the first line thereof by striking out the words "county commissioners" and inserting in place thereof the words "said state board." **Amendment. P. S. 220, § 71.**

SECTION 12. This act shall take effect on the first day of July in the year eighteen hundred and ninety-seven, provided that the members of said board may be appointed at any time after the passage of this act, and may appoint agents and officers and assign their duties before the said first day of July. **When to take effect.**

An Act in relation to issuing to prisoners permits to be at liberty.

Be it enacted, etc., as follows:

Amendment of St. 1884, c. 255, § 33.

Section 1. Section thirty-three of chapter two hundred and fifty-five of the acts of the year eighteen hundred and eighty-four is hereby amended in the first and second lines thereof by striking out the words "commissioners of prisons" and inserting in place thereof the words "state board of prison commissioners," and in the third and fifth lines thereof by striking out the word "they" wherever it occurs therein and inserting in place thereof the word "it" and by striking out the following words in said section, "*provided, however*, that no permit shall be issued to a person transferred or removed from the state prison to said reformatory except with the approval of the governor and council," so that said section when amended shall read as follows: "*Section 33.* When it shall appear to the state board of prison commissioners that any person imprisoned in said reformatory has reformed, it may issue to him a permit to be at liberty during the remainder of his term of sentence upon such conditions as it deems best, and it may revoke said permit at any time previous to its expiration. The violation by the holder of a permit granted as aforesaid of any of the terms or conditions of such permit or the violation of any of the laws of this Commonwealth shall of itself make void said permit."

Amendment. St. 1887, c. 435, § 2.

Section 2. Section two of chapter four hundred and thirty-five of the acts of the year eighteen hundred and eighty-seven is hereby amended in the first and second lines thereof by striking out the words "governor and council" and inserting in place thereof the words "state board of prison commissioners," and in the third, fifth and sixth lines thereof by striking out the word "they" wherever it occurs in said lines and inserting in place thereof the word "it," so that said section shall read as follows: "*Section 2.* When it shall appear to the state board of prison commissioners that any person sentenced to the state prison as an habitual criminal has reformed, it may issue to him a permit to be at liberty during the remainder of his term of sentence upon such conditions as it deems best, and it may revoke said permit at any time previous to its expiration. The violation by the holder of a permit granted as aforesaid of any of the terms or conditions of such permit or the violation of any of the laws of this Commonwealth shall of itself make void said permit."

SECTION 3. Section three of chapter four hundred and thirty-five of the acts of the year eighteen hundred and eighty-seven is hereby amended in the third and fourth lines thereof by striking out the words "governor shall issue his warrant" and inserting in place thereof the following words "state board of prison commissioners shall issue an order," and in the fifth line thereof by striking out the word "warrant" and inserting in place thereof the words "order of arrest," so that said section as amended shall read as follows: "*Section 3.* When any permit granted under the provisions of the preceding section has been revoked or has become void as aforesaid, the state board of prison commissioners shall issue an order authorizing the arrest of the holder of said permit and his return to said state prison. Said order of arrest may be served by any officer authorized to serve criminal process in any county in this Commonwealth. The holder of said permit when returned to said state prison as aforesaid shall be detained therein according to the terms of his original sentence, and in computing the period of his confinement the time between his release upon said permit and his return to the state prison shall not be taken to be any part of the term of sentence."

Amendment. St. 1887, c. 435, § 3.

SECTION 4. Section one of chapter four hundred and forty of the acts of the year eighteen hundred and ninety-four, as amended by chapter two hundred and fifty-two of the acts of the year eighteen hundred and ninety-five, is hereby amended by striking out the thirteenth line thereof.

Amendment. St. 1894, c. 440, § 1.

SECTION 5. Section two of chapter five hundred and four of the acts of the year eighteen hundred and ninety-five is hereby amended in the ninth and tenth lines thereof by striking out the words "without the approval of the governor and council nor."

Amendment. St. 1895, c. 504, § 2.

SECTION 6. This act shall take effect upon the first day of July next.

Appendix G.

An Act to provide for the appointment of a probation officer for the superior court.

Be it enacted, etc., as follows:

Chief justice of superior court may appoint probation officer, etc.

Section 1. The chief justice of the superior court may, if in his judgment it be deemed best, appoint one person to perform the duties of probation officer within the city of Boston under the jurisdiction of said court. Said probation officer shall hold his office during the pleasure of the said chief justice, and shall be subject to and governed by all the provisions of chapter three hundred and fifty-six of the acts of the year eighteen hundred and ninety-one and of all other laws affecting probation officers, in so far as the same may be applicable thereto.

Clerk of superior court for Suffolk to give notice of appointment.

Section 2. The clerk of the superior court for the county of Suffolk shall, when an appointment is made under this act, forthwith notify the commissioners of prisons of the name of the officer so appointed.

Act not to conflict with St. 1891, c. 356, § 7.

Section 3. The provisions of this act shall in no way conflict with the provisions of section seven of said chapter three hundred and fifty-six.

Section 4. This act shall take effect upon its passage.

An Act to provide for the appointment of an additional woman probation officer in the municipal court of the city of Boston.

Be it enacted, etc., as follows:

Chief justice of municipal court of Boston to appoint additional woman probation officer.

Section 1. The chief justice of the municipal court of the city of Boston may appoint an additional probation officer, who shall be a woman, and who shall be governed by all the provisions of chapter two hundred and seventy-six of the acts of the year eighteen hundred and ninety-two.

Section 2. This act shall take effect upon its passage.

Appendix H.

An Act to abolish the payment of a fine as a punishment for drunkenness.

Be it enacted, etc., as follows:

Section 1. Section five of chapter four hundred and twenty-seven of the acts of the year eighteen hundred and ninety-one, as amended by chapter three hundred and three of the acts of the year eighteen hundred and ninety-two and by chapter four hundred and forty-seven of the acts of the year eighteen hundred and ninety-three, is hereby amended by striking out all of said section after the word "file" in the twentieth line thereof. Amendment. St. 1891, c. 427, § 5.

Section 2. This act shall take effect upon its passage.

www.ingramcontent.com/pod-product-compliance
Lightning Source LLC
Chambersburg PA
CBHW030546270326
41927CB00008B/1538